IN POWER TO EMPOWER

IN POWER TO EMPOWER

6 ENTREPRENEURIAL LEADERSHIP PRINCIPLES

AFROZE ALI

NEW DEGREE PRESS

COPYRIGHT © 2020 AFROZE ALI

All rights reserved.

IN POWER TO EMPOWER

6 Entrepreneurial Leadership Principles

ISBN   978-1-64137-444-6   *Paperback*

          978-1-64137-445-3   *Kindle Ebook*

          978-1-64137-446-0   *Ebook*

CONTENTS

ACKNOWLEDGEMENTS

———

First and foremost, I would like to acknowledge and express gratitude for the blessings in my life from Allah, our Creator and Sustainer. I consider it a blessing to serve my community where I get many opportunities to learn a lot about leadership. Special shoutout to IPN.

To my mom and dad: thank you for giving me the best that life has to offer. Everything I am today is because of you, your love, your hard work, your support, your prayers and your unwavering sense of ethics and faith in our Creator. I am proud to be your daughter, and I offer this book to our Creator and the world as a part of your legacy.

To my husband and partner in life, Alykhan Samji. I say: thank you for seeing me as an equal. You see the best in me, especially when I doubt myself. You have provided an incredible amount of moral support, as well as bearing the responsibilities of our home and family while I focused on completing this book. We learned about the word "empower" together, and I am extremely blessed that we can practice empowerment by empowering each other.

To the entire Samji family: thank you for empowering me, your daughter-in-law and sister-in-law, to go after all my dreams.

To one of my oldest and closest friends, Angela Abalos: your support has been incredible from when we were in the 4th grade all the way until now. You've seen me grow the way a sibling would and I am grateful for having you in my life. Also, thank you for being my ultimate proofreader and sanity checker. I could not have done this without your positivity.

I would also like to take this opportunity to thank my interviewees and subject matter experts who shared their time and their experiences with me: Dr. Asif Ashiqali, Zubair Talib, Victoria Platt, Christina Lagoda, Maureen Blandford, Alykhan Samji, and Dr. Lynn Huynh.

If I have missed anyone in these acknowledgements, please forgive me, but know that everyone I have met has an impact on me, whether consciously or unconsciously. Thank you to everyone who has been in my life and has contributed to it.

I have been incredibly blessed by having over 50 people support this book as Early Supporters and Beta Readers without even reading a single page: they believed in me and gave me the strength to get this book to the finish-line, and that too in the middle of a pandemic. Thank you for believing in me. **All of my Early Supporters and Beta Readers are listed in the following pages. Thank you all again.**

Finally, I would like to acknowledge my ancestors and the land of my forefathers of the Indian Subcontinent. I am incredibly proud of my heritage and have believed wholeheartedly that this great-granddaughter of farmers and lower social castes would finally have a voice. This is for the mothers, grandmothers and sisters who came before me who did not have a voice. **We will speak now and we will rise up.**

EARLY SUPPORTERS AND BETA READERS

Aamir Bhojani
Ahmad Noordin
Alice McGinley-Taylor
Alykhan Samji
Angela Abalos
Arsalan Aslam
Asad Abdulla
Asif Ashiqali
Asiya Bari
Asma Bhaidani
Asma Hooda
Ayaz Parbtani
Azim Saju
Christina Lagoda
Ebrahim Valliani
Eric Koester
Faizan Sabzaali
Farah Manjiyani
Fatima Hooda
Haider and Almas Samji
Insiyah Jamal
Jenn MacKenzie Jacobs
Jennie Fronczak
Julie McCoy
Kristine Irene Mae
Liz Vydra
Lynn Foucrier
Maniza Ahmed
Mark Rosal
Maureen Blandford
Mehrab Momin
Mehreen Kassam
Monica Georgescu
Naaz Samji
Nadeem Panjwani
Najiba Keshwani
Nimira Samji
Noshin Jamal
Rak Singh
Rani Ali
Rozina Hirani
Sabrina Lakhani
Salima Kapadia
Salimah Samji

Samir Basaria

Sarah Daya

Sehare Hemani

Shaan Merchant

Shahina Virani

Shahzil Shamshuddin

Shakeel Mohamed

Shehzad Inayat Ali

Shenila Babool

Simran Ali

Soni Dhami

Stephanie Hopper

Tameez Sunderji

Tony Steel and Brooke

Smith of SMITH

Victoria Beswick

Zarin and Farhad Ali

Ziya Shah

Zubair Talib

INTRODUCTION

——

This book is not about women's rights or diversity.

The issue of leadership, undoubtedly, greatly impacts the lives of women—whether at home, in the workplace, or other public spheres. It's important to remember, however, that it's not specifically a woman's issue. It's a larger issue that afflicts everyone and factors into how individuals conduct business and lead groups of people.

Also, this book is not about diversity but about how a lack of diversity, and a lack of pluralistic viewpoints, holds us back from moving forward and having a growth mindset.

Gender played a role in my perception of my own leadership skills, among other factors, such as my perceived lack of experience. Some things are systemic problems and other things I might have simply convinced myself to be the truth. The role of this book is to tear apart our notions of leadership and power—how we learn about it and how we can readjust our perceptions.

WHAT IS A LEADER?

A leader is someone who can influence another person in the way they think or behave, and direct that person to take action in a specific manner. I may see a leader different from the way you or anyone else might. Later in this book, I explore how we learn about power and leadership through the course of our development and how we inherit leadership skills from those who have led us in the past.

ABOUT ME

I would like to share things about my background that can't be found in my LinkedIn profile. I am the great-granddaughter of farmers and laborers from the Indian subcontinent. I am the granddaughter of shopkeepers and salaried employees. During my formative years, I was the daughter of a taxi driver and a housewife.

Culturally, I learned early on what my role was supposed to be. I was expected to be a quiet girl and that I was, at least on the outside. I appeared to be poised, cool, calm, and collected...mature even. And I was only three years old! Some would say I could attribute this to being an only child and hanging out with adults. This probably had a lot to do with it.

My mind, however, was wild and loud and creative and imaginative. I daydreamed all the time, often imagining situations where I was outspoken and in charge. Many times, I even dreamed up embarrassing comedy sequences in which my grade school bullies ended up with pie on their faces. Sometimes I would start laughing out loud during class, and it only made my reality worse for me.

Before I continue, I would like to emphasize that I love my parents and am grateful to them for *everything* they have done for me and given me. I can never repay them for their unconditional love. I am sure that some aunty or uncle will quote something from this book out of context to make my parents feel bad. To them, I will say, "Just put the book down now; you're missing the point entirely."

I share things in this book I have reflected on about myself, my upbringing, my work and volunteer environments, my colleagues, and my friends. It's not meant to be a criticism of the people in my life but rather a summary of insights I use to learn about myself and improve who I am as a person and a leader. **Both my parents and I have gone through a great deal of personal growth since I was a young child, and we're all better people for it.**

Other kids' parents, much to my dismay, loved me to pieces and would ask my parents how they made me so "nice." My dad would respond, "Kids are watching your every move. So they can spot a hypocrite a mile away. Never tell your kids to do something that you don't do yourself."

My dad was not the cool, quiet, calm, and collected one; my mom was, and her role in the family was made very clear to me by our family dynamics: she was not the leader. So, yes, I learned by watching my parents, but not necessarily the parent my dad ever acknowledged I was watching. The primary decision-maker was supposed to be my dad, even in areas where women traditionally had the supposed expertise.

While this still wasn't enough to teach little Afroze about leadership and gender roles, this next example is one of many that made it very clear.

When I was in grammar school, I taught my dad the pledge of allegiance. He was not happy when I told his friends that I taught it to him. At that point in my life (I was about ten), I was an expert at it. My parents are immigrants to the United States, so they didn't learn this growing up. I was taught, however, not to take credit for teaching it to him and to never bring it up in public again because it embarrassed my dad. However, when it came to my mom, he embarrassed her in public all the time and claimed credit for things she had done. I observed from our family dynamics that his pride mattered, but mine and my mom's didn't.

He also took pride in the fact that he educated me, moving heaven and earth to pay the fees, at some of the best private schools in the city. My mom spent *countless* hours helping me with homework and driving me to and from school and all my extra-curricular activities. Of course, to friends and family, he claimed to have educated me himself. My parents both contributed to my upbringing equally—my father financially and my mother with time, care, and attention. I paid attention to my dad's language, how he awarded (and didn't award) credit and recognition, and how financial contribution was given more importance than other types of contribution. I also observed my mother's response to these declarations. She continued to give him credit and downplay the part she played in my upbringing.

My dad's leadership style had set me up to always downplay myself, my accomplishments, and my sense of independence while having a hyper-stimulated mind. I was supposed to be a prim and proper young lady on the outside, a girl who only spoke when she's spoken to, with a mind full of ideas and imagination with nowhere to go. This was only made worse when these same expectations extended to other young women in the family and in my friends' family.

My parents learned what was right and wrong from their parents, and my grandparents learned it from their parents, and so on. Where was the disconnect? Well, my parents came to the United States in the seventies and eighties from the Indian subcontinent. I use the term "Indian subcontinent" because, culturally, my dad feels Pakistani and my mom feels Indian. Before the partition, my grandparents had never even heard of Pakistan because it did not yet exist. The confusion in our home was real.

The United States had already experienced significant social changes such as the Civil Rights Movement and the women's liberation era of the 1960s. I definitely can't summarize the temperature of social change in India and Pakistan in a couple of sentences. India has been a little more progressive than Pakistan, as it pertains to female empowerment. Even that has happened recently, within the past decade. I gauge India's progressiveness by the topics that the Bollywood film industry chooses to tackle. In addition to learning about Indian history in school, most Indians who have never lived in India learn everything they know from Bollywood movies. Bollywood has recently been depicting women as strong, independent, smart characters. My parent's favorite

Bollywood movies tend to have fragile, traditional Indian female characters with strong, intelligent, in-charge male characters. My parents were raised believing in a completely different set of gender politics than what my western education was telling me was possible in the West.

I always argued that I wouldn't be treated this way if I were a boy. My dad vehemently disagreed, but his actions said otherwise. I was the picture-perfect daughter who had to be humble...even if my dad wasn't. This demeanor was respected by a community of people who thought just like he and my mom did. Heck, even my mom thought it was better to "zip the lip" instead of being confrontational.

I learned from my childhood that men were allowed pride, hypocrisy, and decision-making authority over their own lives *and the lives of others*, particularly the women in their lives. Women needed to be entirely perfect and invisible.

These lessons set the stage, terribly, for what was to come.

This book is about leadership, right? I'm getting there. While this isn't a book about gender roles and women's rights, it was very difficult for me—and I'm sure many other women who have fought gender norms in a Western society—to have any self-worth at all.

I was *conscious and "woke" enough to know I was supposed to have self-worth.* But I was convinced by cultural norms in my younger years that I did not deserve it because of my gender. I was light-years away from being a leader of any kind. Funny thing is, I probably have *tons* of stories of leadership qualities

I acquired from childhood through my early adult years that I never thought were important enough to talk about.

I didn't have much exposure to female leadership until high school. Culturally, "leading" just wasn't something women did. Excelling at home was meant to be the norm, nothing to brag about. You were expected to be humble.

When women excelled outside of the home, people thought they were probably neglecting their expected responsibilities (home-related tasks, children, spouse, etc.). You definitely didn't draw attention to or pursue any achievements unrelated to your family if it meant compromising your gender-specific role. So what if you got all A's and wrote for the school newspaper and won the tennis championship? You didn't clean your room, and learning skills like that were important to having a successful future marriage. Because that was the ultimate goal, right?

In my family, as a woman, you went to school to raise smart children. That's it. That's all we knew as a family. We lived in a joint family in the earliest years of my life, with four adult men and four adult women. My mom was the only formally educated adult in our household, and she wasn't considered a family leader because she was not a man.

Not only was I not supposed to be a leader outside of the house, but I also wasn't expected to have a career in the long run.

I decided to reject that idea altogether. I didn't know how to do it at the time, but I wouldn't become one of the invisible women that my family had considered so long to be the ideal future for virtuous women.

Life could have looked very different for me. I lived at home during college but moved away for my first job after graduation. That's when the proposals—or *rishtas,* as they are called in Southwest Asian families—started pouring in. Apparently, having a job was great, according to my parents, since I had student loans to pay, but life after that was unknown. To my parents, or at least my dad, I was meant to get married and leave my job. From there, my husband would take care of me.

It wasn't long before I got the most ridiculous of marriage proposals. A young man, originally from India, was working in Chicago. My dad loved him. The last time my parents visited India, they spent a lot of time with this gentleman and his family. As a result, when he moved to Chicago, my parents would invite him for dinner, especially during religious festivals. He did not have family in town, and my parents wanted to help him feel at home. I had never met him because I lived in Columbus, Ohio.

I don't remember what my mom thought because she never shared her opinion. She just said, "Daddy knows best." My so-called future in-laws already had my life planned for me. My future husband would remain in the US and work after we got married while I went to India to cook and clean for his mom and whoever else lived in their home.

I was appalled. I did not like this plan for my life, and, more importantly, I wanted to know why these people were making decisions for me? And why was my dad OK with this?

Why did he not stand up for a different future for me? Probably because he thought this arrangement would set me up for life. I had to say no.

After persistently saying no a few times to his marriage proposal, I got a call from this young man's mother. I had never met her before, but she was convinced I was perfect for her son simply because he picked me out of a crowd. She kept repeating that I would never have to work another day in my life. I kept saying, "No, I don't want to do this; I am not interested."

Nobody understood my decision. My dad thought I was letting the proposal of a lifetime slip through my fingers. My mom really wanted me to be happy but publicly stayed quiet. The young man, through all this, only managed to call me once in six months for only ten minutes to discuss the weather.

Here I am over ten years later, more than happy that I decided to say no. I am glad I said, "Not right now" and "not this way." I would be in control of my own fate. No one would decide that for me. There were other options, no matter what people said.

I would lead my life in a different direction. That was the start of my leadership journey.

WHY IS IT SO IMPORTANT FOR ME TO WRITE THIS BOOK?

As I observed the world around me (companies and people), I noticed trends and patterns. I've spotted train wrecks as they were about to happen, powerless to stop them. I felt that the only way to do this was to be in a position of power. I thought that in order to have power, I needed a formal signifier of leadership bestowed upon me (a title, a credential, a testimonial from a client, etc.). I was under the assumption that I needed someone to validate me as a leader to be one and harness the power that came with it.

I have gobbled up information from experts for years on all kinds of topics: leadership, strategy, organizational culture, just to name a few. I wanted to be more than a consumer of knowledge; I wanted to be a contributor. I felt like I was getting passed up for those things and not being seen as a thought leader because I lacked some magical ingredient. *I was not being seen as a leader from the outside because I did not feel like I was worthy yet of being a leader.* In my mind, a leader was someone in their forties or fifties, someone who had led teams of one thousand-plus people or had started a large multi-billion-dollar company. Those people are constantly revered by all, including me!

Only a handful of people could ever do things that grand, but I did not want to do any of those things. I always knew I wanted to impact the world, but I never put a number next to it. In fact, I am often reminded of a story that struck a chord when I was younger and still holds meaning.

The story is about an old man walking along the beach when he noticed someone moving across the sand as if they were dancing. He got closer and noticed a young woman picking up a starfish and throwing it into the ocean. He asked, "Why are you throwing starfish in the ocean?" She replied that the tide was going out and if these starfish didn't make it back into the water, they would die by the time the tide came back in. The old man then said, "There are hundreds of starfish on the beach. How much of an impact can you possibly have?" She responded, "I have at least made an impact on the life of this one."

I took some creative licenses in retelling that story, but the message is the important part: there are 7.5+ billion people in the world. If I could make a difference in the life of at least one person, I would be satisfied.

That brings us back to my struggle to envision myself in a leadership position. I have not had many formal managerial roles in the traditional sense. I have been what I call an accidental entrepreneur. All the companies I had worked on failed for different reasons. I have not been the CEO of a company, nor did I jump at the chance of being one when it arose. Taking all that into account, it's understandable why I still could not see myself as a leader.

I was measuring leadership based on leaders I encountered in the past, not what a leader should be in the future. I have led many cross-functional teams and departments through major projects. I have helped companies dream up entirely new lines of business and revolutionized the way they create experiences for their customers. I have influenced decision-makers in billion-dollar organizations, earned the trust of my colleagues, and I always keep my pulse on what is to come so I can advise clients accordingly. Even though I didn't see myself as a leader, I was doing what all leaders need to do: solve problems using data and foresight with the right amount of collective wisdom from the group of people I was working with.

Some people asked me to provide written feedback on their leadership styles, and as I was writing it, I started to see some trends. It was just a matter of time before I started writing them all down, at first just to gather data but, eventually, to put together data points for this book. The strategist in me has, over time, been thematically categorizing major issues and areas of opportunity within leadership.

I have encountered many examples of leadership in different aspects of my life. In my personal life, I have my family members and friends. Professionally, I have had several great managers and mentors. I share some examples throughout this book, but I wanted to categorize my observations in a directional manner because, well, that's how my brain processes information. I will do this a lot throughout the book, so get ready.

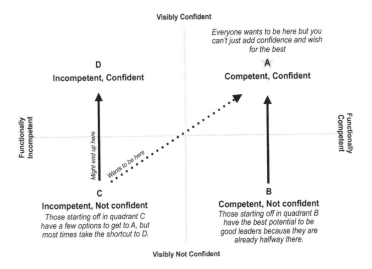

A. Competent and confident
B. Competent and not confident
C. Incompetent and not confident
D. Incompetent and confident

The goal is for everyone to feel like they can be in quadrant A, competent and confident. That is where you have all the experience and knowledge you need while also having the confidence you need to effectively lead people. People in the other quadrants typically wish to be in that quadrant or may falsely believe they are in that quadrant.

For instance, people in quadrant C want to be like the people they see in quadrant A. They have two choices. The first choice is to take the long route by learning what's necessary to be competent (move to quadrant B) then work on their confidence (and then move to quadrant A). More often than not, people make the second choice, where we often see examples of bad leaders: people who have not gained the competence needed to get something done but have enough confidence and charisma to get a formal leadership position. This can also be tied to the psychological term called the Dunning-Kruger effect.[1] This is a cognitive bias that allows people to believe that their abilities are greater than they are. This is related to the cognitive bias known as illusory superiority, which gives people the false belief that they are better than other people, both in terms of personal characteristics and abilities.[2]

You can see how that is very different from being confident in your actual abilities.

If you are in quadrant B, you are probably complacent, or not satisfied with where you are in your career. Trying to push yourself into quadrant A feels like an extremely terrifying and uncomfortable thought. Chances are, if you're reading this book, you may be in quadrant B. The intent is for you to have the tools to see yourself in quadrant A by the end of this book.

I decided I had done a few things that could give me the validation I needed to feel like a leader. As I continued to do research for this book, I was convinced more and more that not only am I a leader, but everyone has a leader in them.

---

1   Daniel R. Ames and Lara K. Kammrath, "Mind-Reading and Metacognition: Narcissism, Not Actual Competence, Predicts Self-Estimated Ability," Columbia.edu, access date 4/25/2020.

2   Justin Kruger and David Dunning, "Unskilled and Unaware of It: How Difficulties in Recognizing One's Own Incompetence Lead to Inflated Self-Assessments," *Journal of Personality and Social Psychology*, 77 (6) (1999): 1121–1134.

THE BOOKSTORE AND THE ANGRY ASIAN WOMAN

I went to Barnes & Noble last year to browse the most popular leadership books.

Out of two shelves filled with ten books about management and leadership, there was only one female author. Even then, it was a co-authored book with the word, "Lies" on the cover. The rest of the shelves were no better; any other books written by women were written for women—a conclusion I based on my very basic knowledge of the use of colors and fonts on book covers.

This moment in the bookstore was monumental for me. Barnes & Noble—a company I generally view as being celebratory of diversity and great visual merchandisers—filled the first two shelves of their "Top Picks in Business" with books by authors teaching the world how to lead while also enjoying the luxury of all kinds of privilege.

While looking at this section, I said out loud, "At least move Brene Brown's *Dare to Lead* to one of the top two shelves labeled "Management and Leadership! It has the word *lead* in the title!"

I eventually had to stop talking to myself, but clearly, I was more than a little irked. I was *annoyed*. I follow *all kinds* of strong, female, business leaders from diverse backgrounds all over social media. They existed. Take Lily Singh's book for example, *How to Be a Bawse*.

Lilly has an analogy in her book about playing video games that really resonates with me, and the theme of this book.

Imagine playing video games that have two players on a screen, and you've been focusing on the wrong character the whole time. This happened to me for almost an entire summer when I played *Mortal Kombat* with a friend. She had mastered pressing all the right buttons when I couldn't even figure out which character on the screen was mine. "You were so confused as to why your controller wasn't working, but, really, you were just trying to control the wrong character. That's what trying to control people is like in real life. We're so often fixated on getting people to behave in accordance with what we want that we forget to focus on ourselves. The best way to stop people from pushing your buttons is to start pushing your own."[3] More on this theme in later chapters.

Lilly is a badass, Canadian woman of Southwest Asian descent. Not only did she write this amazing book, but she recently took over Last Call by Carson Daly. It's called, "A Little Late with Lilly Singh," and I could not be more excited for her entry into late-night television. Asian Americans are making tons of headway in the media, especially in Hollywood.

The business world (that of management, leadership, and business strategy) remains a man's world. While many female leaders exist in the business world, significant roadblocks still prevent women, especially Asian women, from achieving such heights. According to a study of Equal Employment Opportunity Commission data from 2007–2015 in Silicon Valley, Ascend (a nonprofit membership organization for Pan-Asian business professionals in North America), being

---

3   Lilly Singh, *How to Be a Bawse*, (New York: Random House, 2017), 7.

Asian and being a woman is a double-edged sword when it comes to upward movement in one's career. This study looked at several companies, including Apple, Google, Intel, HP, Cisco, Oracle, and Facebook.

One of the biggest findings of this study was that while Asians had become the largest cohort of working professionals, they were least likely among the races to become managers and executives, and women even less so. I have some hypotheses about this which I'll share in future chapters.

Indra Nooyi of Pepsico, Ginni Rometty of IBM, and Mary Barra of GM, among others, are examples of women who made it to the highest ranks of an organization. Were those anomalies or natural paths to leadership paved for future female leaders? Out of five hundred of the Fortune 500, only thirty-three of them are female, and women of color, especially, are missing from this arena.[4]

It's time for a change.

WHAT TO EXPECT IN THIS BOOK?

This book consists of three parts:

The first part of the book looks at where the idea of leadership started through recorded history, how it evolved, and how it was introduced to me when I was a child. I'll share some stories from my childhood and more formative years where

---

4   Courtney Connley, "The Number of Women Running Fortune 500 Companies Is at a Record High," CNBC, May 16, 2019.

I learned about leadership, power, and using emotions to influence people. I also provide a reflection methodology to help you determine your baseline leadership style.

The second part of the book introduces principles of entrepreneurial leadership. These are not principles just for entrepreneurs who want to be leaders but for anyone who wants to apply entrepreneurial concepts to develop their leadership style. I share what I learned from my previous experiences, as well as those of others, on how being a leader is not a destination but a journey. Just as a successful business iterates upon itself and its offerings, a successful leader identifies what is working now and iterates upon what needs to be improved in themselves for long-term success as a leader.

In the third part of the book, I discuss applications of the entrepreneurial leadership principles learned in previous chapters to different types of situations, as well as drawing out examples of how it's all related. For example, when you work on refining parts of your leadership style (e.g., having a better handle of your emotional skills in a professional work setting), it becomes a natural part of your baseline leadership style that can be leveraged outside of work as well. If someone is not empowered in one setting, let's say at the workplace, it impacts how that person feels about themselves elsewhere and vice versa.

This is a book about leadership, written by an Asian woman, for all kinds of leaders. It has been a journey for me, and I hope that you find transformative benefits from it as well.

CUSTOMIZING YOUR BOOK EXPERIENCE

HOW TO GET THE MOST OUT OF THIS BOOK

Treat this book like a map to your own personal and professional development. Here are some suggestions for engaging with this book:

Answer some reflective questions, take notes, and record your responses:

- What have you already learned about both leadership and power?
- What are some doubts you have about yourself? Where did you first start feeling these doubts and when do they feel intensified?
- Do you feel like you should be a leader but are not one? Why do you think that is? How would you define being a leader?
- How will you measure success? Will the result be a new position at your company? Will the result be landing your dream job at a dream company? Will people start asking

you to be a speaker or interview you as an expert? Or will the result be that you finally become your own boss and land that funding for your start-up? Will you accomplish some other goal?

Read the book:
- In the order in which it is organized.
- Do the exercises recommended in Chapter 5 - Assessing Your Leadership and Influencing Baseline.

Once done reading, go back to your responses:
- Review your initial reflections. Highlight areas that stand out.

Make your leadership development plan:
- Analyze your responses to determine what can be a short-term fix versus things you will take longer to improve upon. Also, identify what can be used as opportunities for leadership development.
- Put this information into something like a Gantt chart. You won't accomplish this right away so assign a rough schedule. It's not meant to put pressure on you but to give you an actionable plan to work toward.

Go. Do. Lead.

Disclaimer: I'm not a psychologist, I am not licensed in showing you how to work through major issues.

With the help of a therapist, I continue working through many of the emotions associated with my family, work, relationships, friendships, and my own self-doubt. This book is not meant to replace the help of a professional but complement it. If you're not quite there yet, that's ok. This book can be a start. If you're already working on those things, then this book can help provide a loose structure.

If at any time you feel overwhelmed by the emotions that arise out of reflecting on these things, take a pause, take a breather. These breakthrough moments will help you move forward. They will be uncomfortable sometimes; you may have to go against the grain in your own mind about what has been your truth for many years.

Allow yourself to push your own limits so you can come out on the other side as a newer, more confident version of yourself.

PART ONE

THE CHANGING FACE OF LEADERSHIP

CHAPTER 1

WHAT COMES FIRST, POWER OR LEADERSHIP?

I may have had confusion growing up about my heritage and that of my parents, but here is the reality: knowledge is power. Learning about the politics and colonization of the Indian subcontinent and about Muslim rulers who had a history of ruling peacefully for centuries was a great place to start making sense of where my family might have come from.

Being of Indian descent, I can attest to the fact that no revolution can occur without some level of bloodshed. My family is an example of people impacted by the violence that erupted in post-Independence India against people who did not adhere to the religious ideologies of the nation. However, for purposes of this discussion, we can refer to peaceful revolutions as those with no violence (or relatively very little violence) in order to exert influence and transition power into a new ruling body or rule of law. Can we say that those revolutions were peaceful because of diplomatic conflict resolution? Were the diplomats and powerful even involved in the revolutions? They might have been, but not necessarily on the side one would think of.

What have the most recent peaceful revolutions been trying to accomplish? Life, liberty, and the pursuit of *happiness*? *Power*? By all accounts, all peaceful revolutions were started by those who were in pursuit of *change*. Revolutions throughout human history took place when people were generally unhappy with their current rule and were looking to overthrow the current rule of law, or modify it. To take a closer look at peaceful or nonviolent revolutions, especially contemporary nonviolent movements within the past couple of decades, I looked to learn from Srdja Popovic. Popovic was one of the leaders of the nonviolent movement called Otpor! that removed the Serbian dictator, Slobodan Milošević from power. In his book, Blueprint For Revolution, Popovic discusses how he and his group chose to create a nonviolent movement instead of a violent one. He also goes over the conditions that made Serbia ripe for a movement, one strong enough to overthrow the dictator.

Popovic opens his book by recounting a tour he led for a delegation from Egypt of some landmarks within Belgrade where the Otpor! movement began. What were some of the conditions of the country that made the people so ready for change? Inflation had increased in an impractical way: "the price for two pounds of potatoes skyrocketed from four thousand dinars to seventeen billion in just one year." In addition to that, Serbia was at war with its northwestern neighbor, Croatia, and the economy was crumbling. Speaking out against the government and the policies in place led to severe punishment (getting arrested, beaten up or something more dire altogether). Milošević had taken over all of the academic institutions, such as universities, in addition to the administrative functions of the country. The young people in Serbia did not have much to look forward to in their country. With the economy being so bad, the prospects for getting a job or having a career did not seem realistic.[5]

Popovic and his group had established early on that this would be a nonviolent movement. The reason for this was pretty logical: there was no way Otpor! could compete with Milošević's military and police might. Milošević was not a respected leader; he was a dictator who ruled with fear as described by Popovic, "Milošević's dictatorship, after all, was fueled by fear: fear of our neighbors, fear of surveillance, fear of the police, fear of everything." In the face of fear, Otpor's greatest strength was the use of laughter and fun; they were going to overthrow Milošević by winning over the hearts of the people of Serbia.[6]

Exerting influence with the spread of ideas and rhetoric is an effective method for a peaceful revolution. However, many people have come to believe that only the rich, strong and powerful can influence the masses to bring change. Dictators rely on the masses' capacity to endure oppression UNTIL they start to believe that change is within the reach of a regular,

---

5   Srdja Popovic. *Blueprint for Revolution: How to Use Rice Pudding, Lego Men, and Other Nonviolent Techniques to Galvanize Communities, Overthrow Dictators, or Simply Change the World* (New York: Random House Publishing Group, 2015), 4,7, Kindle.

6   Popovic, *Blueprint for Revolution*, 8,11.

non-elite person. Popovic argues that while we romanticize the lore of warriors who fought wars for nations throughout history, it's the grassroots movements that resulted in long-term changes. Wars, in the recent past, have set the stage for more wars, while peaceful movements set a country up for long-term, impactful change.[7]

What does this have to do with leadership? And what does it have to do with this book? Leaders, at a high level, are trying to do one of three things:

- Maintain the status quo (formal leader such as Milošević, keeping power through dictatorial means, and utilizing tactics like fear and violence).
- Challenge the status quo (People demanding changes to policies or methods of governing such as Otpor!; secondary leader(s) emerge who represent the needs/demands of the people such as Popovic's short time in the Serbian parliament after the fall of Milošević[8]).
- Overthrow the status quo (formal leader loses legitimacy; vacancy in the leadership role that can immediately be filled by leaders who might have been representing the needs of the people or fragmented leadership across groups or cliques; this can tend to happen with violent revolutions, where concrete ideas on how a group or country should be managed after the removal of a leader and so many leaders emerge based on the ideology they represent).

---

7   Popovic, *Blueprint for Revolution*, 22-23.
8   Popovic, *Blueprint for Revolution, Preface*.

All these things can be done using any means necessary. In the past, this would have meant leaders sacrificing life and limb (mostly those of others) to achieve these objectives. If we learn anything about human behavior from the Serbian Revolution, it's that people will willingly follow leaders who appeal to their intelligence through ideas.

It is entirely possible for peaceful revolutions to bring change to a nation. Why is it important to reflect on this? I was not sure what influenced my leadership style. I had fine examples of leaders/managers in my life, so I should have it figured out, no?

Research has found that childhood experiences impact who you become as an adult, but no clear lines are drawn. For instance, if a person develops a response to an experience in their home as a child, that doesn't necessarily mean that they will only behave that way at home as an adult. Everything that we experience during childhood and early adulthood impacts us throughout the rest of our lives. Those experiences helped to shape the person you are right now--your parents, teachers, the media, books you might have read as a kid, that random song you might have overheard waiting for the doctor, your friend from a different ethnic background, and so on.

So how do you tease out leadership lessons from these experiences? If you had to put a nice, neat box around it, it would simply be one person trying to influence another to get a specific response or action. More on this in the next few chapters.

So, it starts like this: Once upon a time, "6 million years ago, a single female ape had two daughters. One became the ancestors of all chimpanzees, the other is our own grandmother."[9]

In order to think about the history of power and leadership, I'll have to do a quick anthropological recap to provide proper context. I rely on the book *Sapiens: A Brief History of Humankind* by Yuval Noah Harari to help inform this recap.

HUMANS: THE BEGINNING

The qualities we look for in a leader, or that we should have as leaders, developed over millions of years. This development is evidenced by Harari in his book. According to archeologists, the earliest humans were hunters and gatherers. They moved around from place to place to find food and shelter. They traveled in a band and competed with other bands for the limited resources around them.[10]

Sometimes, when these bands encountered a foreigner that might pose danger, they worked together to survive[11]. These are the earliest known examples of humans cooperating with each other. For something like that to work, one or a few people led the group, and the rest decided to follow, even if the band or groups of bands did not provide formal political structures[12]. Clearly, it worked because our species did not die out, and we all survived to do things like write this book.

---

9   Yuval Noah Harari, *Sapiens: A Brief History of Humankind* (Canada: Harper Perennial, 2014), 5.

10 Harari, *Sapiens,* 40, 43.

11 Harari, *Sapiens,* 81.

12 Harari, *Sapiens,* 47, 48.

During this time, Harari talks us through what is known as the Cognitive Revolution. During the Cognitive Revolution, humans started sharing more knowledge with each other and developed norms for social relationships. Most importantly, humans started using their imaginations and did not shy away from exchanging ideas with each other. This lay the groundwork for many more things to come.[13]

The Cognitive Revolution was not just about transmitting larger amounts of information to larger groups of people. It was also about some of the wider consequences that resulted from this new human ability. For example, early humans' ability to transmit larger quantities of information resulted in planning and carrying out complex actions such as avoiding lions and hunting bison. This is where our early human ancestors' ability to observe things, spot trends, and identify when and where they might do their best in surviving came into play. In addition to physical survival, larger groups of people learned how to co-exist harmoniously.[14]

More people were able to communicate ideas about the intangible (tribal spirits, nations, human rights, etc.) and started establishing the basis for higher level thinking that went beyond simply solving for the real, the here and the now. This helped humans self-organize themselves in a way like never before, which ultimately planted the seeds for the agricultural revolution, and what is now known as culture.[15]

---

13   Harari, *Sapiens*, 32.
14   Harari, *Sapiens*, 36-37.
15   Harari, *Sapiens*, 32-37.

PLANTING THE SEEDS FOR THE HUMAN RACE

Over time, someone figured out how to grow crops, which benefited humans in so many ways. The agricultural revolution changed the course of history for humans. They no longer had to go place to place to find food. They could plant roots, literally and figuratively. Suddenly, people had more time to think about things like the cosmos, divinity, and their feelings and turn these thoughts into ideology. People's professions diversified, and leaders emerged. Leaders had authority because of power, which came from their ownership of resources, ideology, or military might. This led humans into the era of unification[16].

Here are some examples of large-scale human cooperation systems[17]:

- Widely accepted myths, organized religion, philosophical schools of thought (ideology)
- Political structures, legal systems, and institutions (i.e., empires, law, and order)
- Trade networks, barter, money as a system of mutual trust (resources)

Civilizations learned more formally about leadership through this unification process. Modern civilization evolved from early leadership styles because motivations evolved as well. Just as humans, through the course of their lifetime, have different needs (in a non-linear fashion;

---

16   Harari, *Sapiens*, 100-107.
17   Harari, *Sapiens*, 63-106.

Maslow's hierarchy), so has humanity's needs and motivations evolved over time.[18]

LEADERS OF THE FUTURE AND MODERN POLITICAL SCIENCE

Here is my attempt at summarizing how leadership developed through the course of time. People have always had basic human needs. Early leaders maintained power by having control over and continuing to provide these things. Those who could speak to the metaphysical nature of things gained power among the masses by providing what seemed like logical explanations for inexplicable things (i.e., death, natural disasters, etc.).

A natural hierarchy emerged. Those at the top had the most access to resources (in the form of taxes or some form of sheer expropriation). In some cases, they could make claims to powers from God (divine authority, God Emperor, divine right of kings). Over time, corruption, disparate distribution of wealth, etc. forced a decentralization of power (French and American Revolution) and authority over the utilization of resources (Russian Revolution).

In undergrad, I learned about leaders taking power away from people and accumulating it. These were considered the acts of an effective leader. Truth be told, that might have been an effective way for a ruler to obtain power, but not necessarily an effective way for a ruler to maintain the loyalty of the people. This is evident in the large number of recorded cases

---

18   Harari, *Sapiens*, 163-244.

of revolution throughout history, where the working-class people took power back from the leader.

But in both cases—people taking power from the ruler or the other way around—there is a sort of manipulation. Rulers used fear as a tactic for maintaining their power because they, and their advisers, knew it would work. They understood what made people tick. Revolutions were ignited by new leaders who managed to persuade the masses that their old ruler was ineffective (us vs. them, make people feel cheated and angry).

Modern political science took a closer look at the use of power through emotion, or influence, to rule humans. The Center for Creative Leadership (CCL) summarized influence in three ways[19]:

- Logical appeals
- Emotional appeals
- Cooperative appeals

Logical and cooperative appeals seemed clear. Emotional appeals felt like a grey area to me.

A quick Google search of "emotional intelligence" resulted in 453,000,000 search results (in comparison, another popular search term, cryptocurrency, only has a mere 96,700,000 results). My curiosity started gnawing at me over the years. The definition of emotional intelligence is "the capacity to be aware of, control, and express one's

---

19   "Master the 3 Ways to Influence People," Center for Creative Leadership, accessed July 26, 2020.

emotions, and to handle interpersonal relationships judiciously and empathetically."

However, something did not sit well with me.

Being aware of and in control of one's own emotions, how they're expressed, and handling one's interpersonal relationships judiciously and empathetically seems rather...calculated. Could this not be used for both good and bad?

The example sentence that Google used to demonstrate the use of the term was, "Emotional intelligence is the key to both personal and professional success."

Well, yes, if you know how someone is feeling, and you have an amazing ability to control your own emotions and impulses, you can patiently manipulate them to get what you want, couldn't you?

THE APPEALS AND THEIR CONTEXT

According to the CCL, logical appeals rely on people's rational and intellectual reasons for engaging with someone or something. Emotional appeals connect the objectives of a project or request to someone's individual value systems or long-term goals. Lastly, cooperative appeals rely on people's desire to work together with others in a consultative or collaborative approach.[20] Remember these definitions because you'll need them later.

---

20 "Master the 3 Ways to Influence People," Center for Creative Leadership, accessed April 25, 2020.

I will use these three appeals as the basis to determine one's past and current leadership styles and a good way to determine how to develop one's future leadership style.

Logical and cooperative appeals became more popular ways to lead later through history. Emotional appeals, though, were of particular interest to me, especially as a political science major in college.

Most leaders of the past appealed to the underlying emotion or motivation of self-preservation. They led with fear and terror through feudalism within their countries and colonialism in countries that they started to conquer. It wasn't until the French, American, and, further down the road, the Industrial Revolutions that the intellectuals of the day started questioning the morality of leaders, equality, disparate distribution of resources, and conditions of the working class. The Age of Enlightenment, a time of intellectual and scholarly discourse of the 1700s, generated ideas that undermined the authority of the monarchy and the church and paved the way for the political revolutions of the eighteenth and nineteenth centuries.[21]

WHAT DID THIS MEAN FOR MY LEADERSHIP JOURNEY?

If it isn't apparent yet, I enjoyed learning about history, and I had planned on applying to law school at some point. Law schools preferred people with a political science background, or so I was told. The study of power was particularly

---

21   Eugen Weber, *Movements, Currents, Trends: Aspects of European Thought in the Nineteenth and Twentieth Centuries* (1992).

fascinating to me: how people were manipulated by oligarchs or dictators during peaceful times and how rulers and generals used force to take power away from people during times of war. While I read stories about these things happening over the course of hundreds of years in all parts of the world, I simultaneously saw these types of tactics play out on the world stage and in US politics during the early 2000s (and even more so within the past few years). I also started delving into things like gender politics in college, and many of those topics hit a nerve. Most classes left me angry or sad, or a combination of both. The world seemed like a dire place to be, with everyone trying to grab as much power as possible.

After four years of studying the history of politics, I was convinced that while I enjoyed learning about policy, government, war, culture, and history, I was not interested in a profession based in so much darkness and deception. Those in power were capable of doing anything to maintain their power.

Twelve years later, I find it ironic that I am writing a book about leadership and its relation to power. What happened in those twelve years?

After college, I started working in corporate America and learned about office politics. I often heard people say things like, "I don't like politics," in reference to people using their power to get what they wanted in a corporate setting. I also encountered people using their power for good. That's when my perception started to shift.

The dark side of emotional intelligence has been studied for a long time by philosophers, theologians, and early political scientists. I was particularly interested in looking at the dark side of emotional intelligence because of all the recent focus in professional development within organizations on emotional intelligence.

Not only was I curious now, I was determined to find out how emotional intelligence makes its debut in power-play and why now do we think it's so crucial for leaders to have this characteristic. I was compelled to dust off some of my old books and take another look at Niccolò Machiavelli.

THE PRINCE THAT WAS MACHIAVELLI

Born in Florence in 1469, Niccolò Machiavelli lived through the Italian Renaissance. His most famous writings, namely *The Prince*, gave him a reputation of being cynical and even immoral. In it, he wrote, *"Those who draw pictures place themselves below in the plain to understand the nature of the mountains and other high places, and in order to understand the plains place themselves upon high mountains. Similarly, to understand the nature of the people one needs to be a prince, and to understand princes one needs to be of the people."*

He set the stage very early in his book that there must be an understanding of the "other side." Scholars claim that Machiavelli may have been one of the very first modern political scientists. This school of thought based on *The Prince* is now called Machiavellianism, a view that politics is amoral and that any means, however unscrupulous, can justifiably be used in achieving political power.[22]

Call it a political philosophy or an area avidly studied by psychologists, but one must admit that it's fascinating. Kashmira Gander, of *Newsweek,* wrote in May 2019 that, "Modern research found that Machiavellianism is negatively related to emotional intelligence, though Machiavellianism is related to using emotional manipulation (i.e., making another person feel embarrassed, ashamed or feel guilty). However, emotional intelligence is often associated with pro-social behavior. Therefore, people with Machiavellianism may use a "darker" aspect of emotional intelligence to manipulate others for their own gain."[23]

Aha! I knew there was a dark side to emotional intelligence. I also started to wonder why a reporter who typically writes about health, gender, LGBTQIA+ issues, human rights, subcultures, music, and lifestyle would suddenly write about the psyche of politicians. Maybe someday, when someone picks up this book from the sale bin at Amazon's brick-and-mortar bookstore, they can chuckle at my pitiful attempt at satire.

But don't worry; this book is not about Machiavellianism. It's about using the right mix of logical, emotional, and cooperative appeals to be an effective leader. It would be easy enough if it was as simple as saying, "33.3 percent across each of those appeals and you're golden." It's not as easy as that, and looking at how the nature of leadership has changed

22   *Merriam-Webster.* s.v. "Machiavellianism (_n._)." Accessed July 27, 2020.
23   Kashmira Gander, "550 Years Since Niccolo Machiavelli Was Born—How to Check How Machiavellian You Are," *Newsweek*, May 3, 2019.

makes the case for why understanding your baseline leadership style is important in evolving into the future leader you hope to become.

This book is also about trying to learn about the prince, figuratively speaking, by being among the people. Whether you've led someone or not, you most certainly have been led at some point. You already have more than enough data points to understand how leadership styles affected you as a follower, and which ones were truly effective in unlocking *your* true potential.

"Nearly all men can stand adversity, but if you want to test a man's character, give him power."

— ABRAHAM LINCOLN

CHAPTER 2

THE POWER TO LEAD

—

*I met an old lady once, almost a hundred years old, and she
told me, 'There are only two questions that human beings have
ever fought over, all through history. How much do you love
me? And who's in charge?*[24]

— ELIZABETH GILBERT, *EAT, PRAY, LOVE*

I didn't feel like a leader because I felt powerless. I felt powerless because I felt like I was voiceless. And owning your voice is hard to do.

Leadership styles are a manifestation of how power is experienced through one's life: blatant/explicit power and latent/implied power. How did my view of power develop over time?

One of my very good friends, Dr. Lynn Huynh, interviewed me for a class assignment back when she was in grad school. She asked me a number of questions but started off by asking

---

24 Elizabeth Gilbert, *Eat, Pray, Love*, (London: Bloomsbury Publishing, 2007), 165.

me to think of people, real or fictional, who had an impact on me. She provided some guidelines on how to pick these people, and this table summarizes the person and the age at which they started making an impact on me:

Approximate age of first contact that had impact	Knew Personally	Real People Through Media	Fictional People Through Media
3	Dad		
4 to 5			Lucy Ricardo
5		Peter Jennings	
8		Oprah	
11			Scout, *To Kill a Mockingbird*
13	Friend		

While the people I chose and my responses were originally from the interview around 2008, I updated the responses to be more relevant to who I am now. One of the questions was, "How did this person lead you to question power?"

Let's take a quick look at my strongest childhood influences. My parents definitely played a big part in my perception of power. I also learned a lot from media personalities and characters in books.

FATHER AND FOREFATHERS

As with everything else, my first introduction to power came from my parents. My dad, in this case, used to say a lot of things about the government and society.

Perhaps because we're an immigrant family, he constantly said the government always comes first, in a good way. He would always tell me, "It's important for you to know that. We have to respect the government that we have here in the US."

He would say this because the government in the country he was from wasn't as good to its people. As I stated, my mom and dad's families are from the Indian subcontinent. My forefathers were from India. Due to the post-colonial partition of India and Pakistan of 1947 and religious persecution in India, my family associates itself with Pakistan a little more. Culturally, though, we are still figuring ourselves out. The governments of India and Pakistan, though, are probably more alike than they'd like to admit. I could fill chapters with the number of examples of why both governments are corrupt, why the politicians are corrupt, how there is rampant bribery, and so on. The people in those countries cannot always rely on the government as people might be able to in other countries. However, both are fairly new democracies, so they are still experiencing some growing pains. (I highly recommend watching comedian Vir Das' "For India" for both a chuckle and a history lesson.)

This was the start of my learning about power. Two governments, one that used its power for the benefit of people and another that used its power for the benefit of the politicians. I don't think my dad thought the system was perfect in the United States, but he feels a sense of patriotism. This is his home. But there was power in the law of the land and that law needed to be followed, for fear of penalty/punishment.

Similar to his respect for the government (Uncle Sam as he always calls it) and always following the laws of the land, he assumed that role in our household. He was the most powerful person in the house, and his rules had to be followed by everyone. He extended his jurisdiction to any blood relative. I'm sure his siblings have their own stories to tell. I started to make many parallels between the government's law of the land and my father's rules of the house, neither of which could be broken, for fear of punishment.

My earliest memory of this was when I was four years old. My parents had dropped me off at my uncle's house so they could attend a religious service. This was a monthly occurrence, and I looked forward to it because, *after* the service, my parents would take me to my favorite park with my favorite lunch, fish and chips. My uncle stepped out to pick up some milk for me, and my cousin was still asleep that early in the morning, so I wandered off to go play with the neighbor's kids. When my parents came back, my uncle had come back and my cousin was awake, but I was nowhere to be found. They finally figured that I must have gone to the neighbor's house to play because they had a little girl about my age. When everyone finally found me, my dad asked me who gave me permission to go next door. I lied and said that my cousin said I could go. Of course, my dad verified with my cousin and she said she was asleep and didn't even know I had come over yet.

I was in trouble for lying for the first time. I did not get my day at the park, and I was forced to eat Indian food for lunch, again. Adult-me wouldn't have minded eating Indian food, but four-year-old me was in a lot of emotional pain. I did not like being punished. I wouldn't lie again any time soon.

PETER JENNINGS – POWER STRUGGLE

Peter Jennings also influenced my view of power. Jennings was a reporter on the nightly news. It was ritualistic to watch his news report through my entire childhood during dinner, right before *Wheel of Fortune*. In his reports, I saw a lot of power struggles: the rich versus the poor, the powerful countries versus the not powerful countries, countries that had oil (or other resources) versus countries that didn't.

He brought to life so many different things, but in each of those instances, there was always a power struggle. If a crime was committed, then the person who held the weapon held the power over the victim, who was powerless and had no means of defending themselves. The rich had power and wealth. Their wealth was their power versus the poor, who have neither; because they don't have wealth, they don't have power. All of his stories had power struggles. It helped me a lot to see live examples of it. In my own life, I couldn't see it as clearly as night and day, but the news helped me see it in a much bigger light.

OPRAH – POWER THROUGH WEALTH AND INFLUENCE

I think Oprah is a powerful person. I used to watch her show when it came on at 9 a.m. when I was off from school, and I used to take a lot of pride in the fact that she filmed her show in my hometown of Chicago. I wish I'd gotten a chance to go see her live. I learned about Oprah's power in two ways. The first was that she was, and is, very wealthy. She did not always have wealth, though, and that only added to her appeal for me. It made people like me feel like a normal person could work hard and become successful.

In addition to her wealth, she had the power of the spoken word. Seeing a powerful woman on TV, someone who said things and had people listen, someone who had a team of people who *worked for* her, seemed impossible to me. But it wasn't, and she existed! But her power was particularly impactful because she used it to help people. While I know she has had tons of producers and writers, something about *her* made her so successful because she had control over, or exuded power over, the way she spoke.

An example of this is Oprah's Book Club. Once she endorsed a book (or really anything at all), the book's sales would skyrocket. Toni Morrison was a literary genius even before she gained popular attention, but Oprah endorsing some of her lesser-known work changed the course of the book's mark on history. According to *Quartz*, the online news publisher, Morrison's book, *The Bluest Eye*, was first published in 1970, and it sold just 2,000 copies. After being featured as an Oprah's Book Club pick in 2000, it sold 800,000 copies.[25]

My opinion of Oprah hasn't changed much since then, but I would probably add Ellen to my list of influential people in the media as well. She certainly wields just as much power and influence through all forms of media (probably even more broadly than Oprah did, since many channels like YouTube and Facebook didn't exist back then).

---

25 Jamilah King, Inae Oh, and Kiera Butler, "Oprah's Book Club Changed the Game—and Created a New World for Black Readers Like Me," Mother Jones, Nov. 1, 2019.

SCOUT FINCH – INJUSTICE, POWER, RECONSIDER THE LEGITIMACY OF THE GOVERNMENT

Oh, Scout. Jean Louise's "Scout" Finch was one of the main characters in the book *To Kill a Mockingbird*. The entirety of the slave trade, institutionalized racism, and all the gigantic ripples it had on an entire group of people was unbelievable to me. I could not wrap my head around it. The book was one of those books you couldn't help but remember for a long time after reading it. Many books have made an impact on me, but the character of Scout Finch has stayed in my memory even now.

The book was all about power. Tom Robinson, who had been falsely accused of raping a poor white woman, had absolutely no power. His place in society was defined by the color of his skin. The rest of society was misusing their power, and the justice system was completely flawed because of this. Scout represents the voice of reason, questioning the system when the status quo accepted the injustices as the norm. My sense of power was initially established through my dad's respect for the government. This sentiment was thrown out of the window because of this book, this character, Scout Finch. While it was a fictional story, it was a strong critique of the time in which it was written. Here was a government condoning the institution of slavery, and I was completely enraged by it.

And now? It still affects me the same way.

LUCY RICARDO – POWER IMBALANCE; MOM'S FAVORITE TV SHOW; HER HAPPY PLACE

I Love Lucy was a show in the United States from the 1950s. The household in the show reminded me of my childhood household in the 1990s. 1950s American culture was a very conservative one, where the men worked to earn money and women stayed home to take care of the home and the children.

Lucy Ricardo was a character in the show. Lucy, a supposedly red-haired woman (we never really saw her hair until the show went from black and white to color) tries to become a star with her show business husband, Ricky Ricardo. The show's setting starts off in a New York City apartment, run by Lucy and Ricky's best friends, Fred and Ethel Mertz.

Lucy and Ethel were always getting themselves into trouble. Most of the time, they were trying to ensure that they didn't get caught by their husbands or by some other party. Their scheming was usually harmless but demonstrated the lengths these women had to go to get their way. Lucy was especially portrayed as childlike, making irresponsible decisions, and getting scolded by her husband, who was clearly the adult.

The show catered to the audience at the time and, in doing so, decided that her husband had the power in the house; he had all the power over the money, how they were to raise their son, and where they were to live. This felt so much like how my family functioned. I thought it was normal. It was forty years before my family existed in the 90s, so it influenced my opinion of American households.

Only when I hung out at my friends' homes did I notice that things were no longer like they were in the 1950s in American households. And now? Now, I completely disagree with all of it. It's just a different reality right now, but you always need something to compare it with. So that's what this show and this character meant to me.

My mom found joy in this show because she could find solace in another woman's situation and laugh at her antics. It was her escape from her reality, and it made her feel like she wasn't alone. It also created a sense of normalcy for her in a domestic environment that she knew wasn't always the easiest.

WHY DID I THINK THIS WAS IMPORTANT TO SHARE?

I originally decided to write a book to explore *why* I could not see myself as a leader. With leadership so inextricably linked to power, there was no way to learn about one without learning about the other.

I recently spoke with one of my mentors, Victoria Platt, an Integration & Transformation Executive at IBM. She said something so important that I asked her if I could share it in this book. I met her back when I worked at Accenture's Innovation Network around 2012. She came in as a subject matter expert on retail experience innovation. I was in complete awe of her and had decided back then that I wanted to be her when I grew up. During our recent conversation, she shared something that I was surprised to hear because, in my mind, she seemed to have it all figured out:

"I had really let other people influence me and intimidate me, and I don't know why I gave them such power. That's probably my biggest mistake. And when you don't understand what gifts you bring, and the power you do bring and what your contribution really is, then you think you're a poser, a loser, and that you'll be found out. Someday, they'll realize I don't belong here. And women do that all the time."

I wrote this part of the book moments after speaking with her. I immediately felt a weight lift from my chest. I have been feeling a lot like this for the past decade. I only recently started to believe that my uniqueness was actually my strength. I was letting people like women in my religious community, my parents' friends, and even some family members have power over me and how I felt about myself.

I could not see myself as a leader because I was waiting for those who were important to my formative years to validate me as a leader. But if their standards for me were never high to begin with, that validation would never happen, leaving me feeling unnecessarily powerless.

It was time to let go and lead myself into my own future.

CHAPTER 3

THE PATRIARCHY, THE BIGOTRY, AND THE INSECURITY

THE PATRIARCHY, MAN

There was no way I could write a book about leadership or career journeys without an homage to women in leadership. I must give a nod to all those who have come before me and ensure that women who come after understand how difficult the road has been. And, of course, it's important for me to acknowledge that I, too, am a leader who is a woman.

There are a few ways to approach this topic.

One way is to assume that the world is actively against women and that is why not enough women are in leadership right now. This approach requires digging into the deepest, darkest depths of the human condition to conclude that everyone is misogynistic. Making this assumption would imply that men hate women and women hate women, and we're all going hell. According to former Secretary of State Madeleine Albright, "There is a special place in hell for women who don't help other women."[26] This makes me laugh and cry at the same time, because I have met my share of women who'd rather see other women burn than to see them succeed.

I stumbled upon a book at the Evanston Public Library in 2019 called *Women and Power* by Mary Beard that puts many of these sentiments into words. I learned that my dad and other men silencing women in public was what men have been taught for centuries. Mary Beard goes as far back as the foundations of Western literature and finds numerous examples of how women were constantly muted or silenced by men, being ordered to return to the private spaces of their lives and leave the public oration to the men. Even if women in the past spoke or were in leadership roles, they were doing so only representing other women. Men would never accept a woman representing them publicly. Comparisons are then made to how women are treated culturally in public debate within the media and by men in power.[27]

While I believe that women and men can both get in the way of women succeeding in the workplace and the public sphere as a whole, the only way to a potential solution is to look at things more objectively.

---

26 Madeleine Albright, Keynote Speech at *Celebrating Inspiration* Luncheon with the WNBA's All-Decade Team, *ESPN.com*, 2006, accessed July 27, 2020.

27 Mary Beard, *Women & Power*, (New York: Liveright Publishing, 2017), 3-45.

Tomas Chamorro-Premuzic—Chief Talent Scientist at Manpower Group and a professor of business psychology—shares in his book, *Why do so many incompetent men become leaders? (And How to Fix It)* how, statistically speaking, women have a harder time becoming leaders because, despite being equally as competent as men, women do not demonstrate the same type of overconfidence that so many male leaders do. This overconfidence in male leaders, according to Chamorro-Premuzic, is always mistaken for competence, but that is rarely the case.[28]

Because women must put more work into achieving the same things as men, they are more intentional. They take leadership roles assuming they don't know enough, or, wanting to appear humble, they claim that they don't necessarily have all the information to start making major changes/decisions.

Traditionally, because men have been led to believe by systems and society that they are experts on everything, they come in with a certain sense of confidence and feel comfortable jumping right in and start "doing things" without necessarily thinking things all the way through. This is, of course, not true of all men but can generally be found as the modus operandi for male leaders at many failing organizations.

If the stats are that most leaders in major companies are men, and that most people dislike their bosses, then men tend to be bad leaders. Using the same statistic of how many leaders in companies tend to be men and marrying them with

---

28 Tomas Chamorro-Premuzic, *Why Do So Many Incompetent Men Become Leaders: And How To Fix It*, (Boston: Harvard Business School Publishing, 2019), 17-37.

these stats: "Almost every leader wants to make more time for strategic thinking. In one survey of ten thousand senior leaders, 97% of them said that being strategic was the leadership behavior most important to their organization's success. And yet in another study, a full 96% of the leaders surveyed said they lacked the time for strategic thinking."[29] One can assume that men are also not taking the time to be strategic.

One must bear in mind that being in a leadership role, or the C-suite, or in a VP-role is not just a nice name for a task manager. A person in the position has the responsibility to make pretty big decisions about how resources are utilized, the culture that will be instilled, and must be able to deliver results.

How are leaders chosen? How are they measured? How are they rewarded? Can they do wrong? It appears if they're a certain type of leader (white males), they can't do wrong and, instead, get rewarded for exuding confidence instead of competence.

This is the chapter where we explore further why this book is not about women's rights. It's about a lack of diversity in background, thought, socio-economic backgrounds, and more. Also, there is now a new, popular sub-culture to *fear* diversity. This is not good for our homes, our communities, our schools, our businesses, or our country.

THE BIGOTRY

Long before I ever felt as confident and competent as I give myself permission to feel now, I was a young woman trying to figure herself out. This is true for many people, but especially for someone like me. I did not really have many role models to lean on, and if I didn't figure my life out for myself, I had plenty of family members ready to figure it out for me.

My first goal was to become financially independent. That's not to say my parents haven't helped me out whenever I've needed it. After all, I'm an elder millennial and I graduated from college at the start of the recession.

Because of the start of the fall of the economy, it had become close to impossible to find a job. And, unlike who I was in high school, I was not an overachiever in college. I had no idea what I was doing during my university years. I did not have a job lined up for when I graduated. The most exciting thing I was looking forward to at the end of that summer was the chance to be a volunteer at an Alzheimer's Gala and then starting my study abroad program in China.

When my program was coming to an end, I'd just hung up from a conversation with my dad. He drove a taxicab to supplement his income while he worked on finding a full-time network engineering job. He was the overachiever of the family.

The passenger in his taxi overheard our conversation. My dad told this stranger about me, and, somehow, it turned into my first job after college. I spent four years there, learning more than I think I ever would have in any grad school.

The company, twenty years old at the time, pitched itself to me and two other new hires. The founders and the other partners were all aging out and wanted to hire younger people to take over the legacy. The company was relatively small (about fifty people worldwide) but was one of the largest specialty firms in the industry.

So, there I was in 2007—twenty years old, done with college, two liberal arts degrees—moving to Columbus, Ohio from Chicago, Illinois to start my first job. I'd be a broker for trade credit insurance. It was heavy in the B2B space, and I had to get an insurance license in order to sell and train clients on how to administer commercial insurance policies. It was a financial services product at the end of the day. I was an international studies and political science major; what did I know about companies and financials?

The answer was that I didn't. The first two years I was at the company, I worked in the Columbus office. My first few weeks there were nothing short of terrifying. This line of work was *intense*, the urgency of getting things done and doing them right meant the difference between companies having enough to make payroll or closing its doors forever. I learned *a lot* about credit and finances.

I had many great people to look up to in Columbus. The founders of the company were absolutely the most amazing human beings I had ever met. Sure, they had their own quirks, but they were *brilliant*. They were truly Renaissance men. One of them was responsible for instilling the company's culture in us, which he did through a many-hour-long session once a week over pizza on Friday. The tradition had started twenty years ago when it was just the two of them.

I and the other new hires were considered G's, which stood for generation. We were the fifth or sixth generation of young employees right out of college who did not get to automatically buy into the company like the previous employees of the company. Another woman was also Indian, and a young man was of Latin-American descent. Part of me thinks they targeted people who would not otherwise feel like they were good enough for other companies or didn't feel like they fit it anywhere else. The land of the misfit toys.

The horror stories we heard from the other G's who started before us were probably a little exaggerated. In reality, this was a tough line of work, with a complicated product, high-risk decisions, and a sense of urgency with *everything*. I didn't know what I was doing most days, but I learned one thing that kept me hanging on: we were all on a partner track by default. They would not hire us otherwise.

In fact, they called us partners every day. I accompanied senior partners into meetings with C-level individuals at publicly traded companies in my early twenties. We even got a simplified employee pension fund, which doesn't happen if you're a recent college grad! My friends were happy if they even had a job. I had decided early on that I would go above and beyond in my work and outside of my work to make a difference at this company. I would earn the name partner at this firm.

While in the Columbus headquarters, I had a chance to spend time with partners and managing directors from our global offices in China, India, Brazil, Mexico, the UK, France, Belgium, and so many other countries. It was a big company through its extended network. I developed relationships with these individuals and often got offered opportunities to join their teams abroad.

Why am I sharing this story? This job was where I learned how to behave like a partner in a company even when, in name, I was not yet one. I assessed the needs of an organization and decided to do something to impact the bigger picture and the top line by taking matters into my own hands. I got global recognition for the work I did for the company and the industry. This was the same job where the entire global company felt like I deserved to become a partner except for the managing director that I ended up reporting to when I moved back to Chicago. I learned that sometimes the way an employee measures success and the way their bosses measure success can be way off, no matter how formal your performance measurement process. This was also the job where I learned about the few strikes against me that I walked into every company with, depending on who I was reporting to: I was a Muslim woman, who was the daughter of an immigrant.

Because I had started at this company at the beginning of the recession, every company was feeling the pressure to retain customers and to cut costs. Our company was not an exception to this by any means; our company had decided to reduce how much our consultants were traveling. That included me and others...however, we were still responsible for maintaining those relationships.

I put all my energy into figuring out the company's operations, seeing where we could start incorporating digital tools to enhance the experience and get customers to stay with us. Getting new business might not have been the option during these times but retaining them was key.

Over the course of my time there, I worked on revamping the company's customer relationship management (CRM) system. I worked with an outside consultant to create a newsletter, started creating videos to use for marketing in an industry still using fax machines and paper documentation, and worked with our developer to add *numerous* features to an online policy management portal sitting dormant for a while.

The founders of the company *loved* my ideas and my work, as did the other account managers, sales folks, and inside sales team. While I had others helping me get these things done, I was doing the job of a CX Strategist (and I didn't even know it at the time) while also doing the job of a trade credit consultant. I grew in both roles and was given more responsibilities by others in the company.

Two years into my being at the company, I asked to transfer back to Chicago to be closer to my family. That had been the plan all along. I did not know what I had just done, but I learned over the next twelve to eighteen months that this amazing company had a poisonous element in the form of the managing director (MD) who worked out of the Midwest office. I still worked with others in the company, but I reported to this MD, who held all the power to decide my career growth in the company.

The company no longer exists because it was bought out, but the MD's unprofessional and ignorant behavior during my time there has been eating away at me for the past decade. And it influenced how I viewed myself as a leader and as a professional.

The MD was anti-"other." He was a misogynist, a racist, a homophobe, and an Islamophobe. He would say *completely* off-color things in a matter-of-fact way, as if everyone must think this way. He was oblivious to how offensive he was.

One example of how he demonstrated his feelings toward women was how he spoke about his wife in public, around me, and around clients. He would say things like he didn't want his wife working, so he made sure he impregnated her even though she expressed that she didn't want any children. He was proud of being so controlling and manipulative!

Another example of this was when we took a major client to lunch one day. I was the youngest person at the table and one of two people of Asian descent, the other one being from the client's side. The MD made a comment about Muslims being terrorists (and this wasn't the first time he had done that). The entire table went completely silent, and everyone turned their heads to uncomfortably look at me, wondering how I would respond. I blushed and started shoveling food into my mouth. I was in my early twenties, and this person would supposedly influence whether I made partner at the firm. I did not know the right thing to do, so I stayed silent.

I later learned that the client of Asian descent had some harsh words for my MD's boss, the founder of the company, about how the MD behaved. She was offended on my behalf. I remember going back to the office that day after lunch, going into a restroom stall, and crying my eyes out because I felt helpless until I heard about what the client did. She stood up for me. I clearly knew how the MD felt about Muslims many times over.

Eventually, I submitted my appeal to be a partner to the board of our company. Everyone I had ever worked with thought it was a no-brainer to make me a partner...except this MD. He was eventually convinced otherwise, and I got offered a partnership, but how could I sit in the same office as this MD knowing he didn't think I deserved this honor?

I loved everyone else in the company. I had even started to love the work and really own it. I was being given more responsibilities working with some of our major global accounts, still in my early twenties. I even got offered positions in other offices in the US and abroad, under the direction of other MDs. I didn't want to leave Chicago, so I only had one option.

I left. I started over, changing careers four years after college. Forget feeling like a leader; I wasn't even happy in my own skin. I could never really talk about why I left that company initially. I couldn't believe I was even experiencing it. I was in shock.

THE INSECURITY

I needed to unpack a lot of emotions because of this situation. Enough years have passed that I can look at things objectively now. I can look back and see that I had not done anything wrong. What happened to me was unacceptable; however, seeing it once did not necessarily give me the tools to do something different when I encountered it again in future roles.

All I could do when I felt slighted by others was to get angry and emotional. I could not understand why, but unfortunately, I knew I'd be seeing it for the rest of my career.

I did not feel satisfied saying this is a male versus female problem, or an us versus them problem, or a problem of bigotry. I wanted to explore something deeper, especially as I was taking a walk down memory lane for this book.

The data also did not support the idea that men were the primary problem for women, if we considered what happened to me a form of workplace bullying. A workplace bullying survey was done in 2017 in the United States, showing that almost 60 percent of US workers were affected by bullying. It also surprisingly showed that workplace bullying is not equally split between men (70 percent) and women (30 percent) and that women bullied more women than men did (more than 65 percent in both cases).[30]

Behavioral scientist Dr. Pragya Agarwal conducted a study of her own and discovered that women can carry an

---

30 Gary Namie, "2017 WBI U.S. Workplace Bullying Survey," Workplace Bullying Institute, accessed April 25, 2020.

unconscious bias against women.[31] Well, I couldn't disagree with that, considering I experienced this type of bias as well.

So why do men, women, and all kinds of people behave this way?

Just like when we were younger, I attributed people's bullying behavior to their own insecurity or because they might be sociopaths.

LEARNING ABOUT ATTACHMENT THEORY

I reached out to one of my friends, Sabrina Lakhani, a behavioral scientist and fellow strategist. We have often turned to each other to vent about work, community life, and relationship dynamics within our families. We grew up together, but we didn't really talk much until a couple of decades later.

Sabrina is one of the foremost experts on attachment theory, exploring attachment theory as it relates to personal relationships. When we spoke, she shared her views on how this impacts how we relate to others and how we might behave as leaders.

Sabrina also describes **attachment theory** on her blog.[32] It in, she notes each of the types of people who exhibit secure, insecure-anxious and insecure-avoidant tendencies.

---

31   Pragya Agarwal, "Unconscious Bias: Do Women Discriminate Against Women?" LinkedIn, March 1, 2018.
32   Sabrina Lakhani, "Birthing a New Consciousness" (blog), May 25, 2016.

1. The **secure** population is able to exhibit both masculine and feminine traits as needed. They can successfully manage their own needs and those of a partner.
2. There are two types of insecure populations: **insecure-anxious** and **insecure-avoidant**.
3. The **insecure-avoidant** population is mostly men who were raised to be ultra-independent, self-centered, and assertive.
4. The **insecure-anxious** population is mostly women who learned to seek approval and sacrificed their own needs and once for others.
5. The **insecure-anxious** most often attracts an **insecure-avoidant** partner. The relationship causes extreme distress and exacerbates their individual insecurities. This creates a broken relationship.

During our conversation, we talked about how leaders might look at competence and confidence, and whether being male or female had anything to do with how one might approach their own perception of leadership. She noted that it's all related to our attachment styles, which are mostly to related how we were raised, what we were groomed to be, and how we observed people in our families exercise their own attachment styles through familial interactions. Our attachment styles are the lenses we use to see ourselves and their relationship with us, though we don't realize we're doing so.

According to Sabrina and the attachment theory, those who lead with an anxious attachment style don't have confidence even though they might be competent. Statistically, the majority of those with an anxious attachment style are generally women, but many men also fall into this category.

These individuals need many words of affirmation. They need a lot of self-pep talks and boosts to their self-esteem, especially if they are not hearing it from others. They might need to be reminded of their own greatness. They are more likely to rate themselves as less competent than they really are. I could totally see myself in these things, especially when it came to my leadership skills.

On the other side is the avoidant attachment style, which is seen mostly in men because of how they are raised, not just because they are men. Many of these leaders generally rate themselves as more competent than they really are. This is also called an overconfidence bias, which I mentioned previously.

Sabrina confirmed my hypothesis that we lack confidence because of how we were raised and the things we heard about ourselves. Her advice is if your environment won't be supportive of you moving forward and becoming truly confident, you must move forward without it.

The goal for a good leader is to be both competent and confident and develop a sense of security in their attachment style, not anxious or avoidant.

I'm glad I had this conversation with Sabrina mainly to check my own bias. I know of enough people from all kinds of backgrounds who could fall into both the secure and insecure buckets. I needed to stick to the facts and not the baggage of the bias I carry by seeing how women in my family and life have been historically treated.

I would rather be open to the possibility that people are not looking at me with bias. That is the only way the focus will be removed from irrelevant factors and shifted to factors relevant to my ability to be a leader.

CHAPTER 4

ASSESSING YOUR LEADERSHIP AND INFLUENCING BASELINE

———

I learned many things through my formative years and through my early career. I learned how confidence and competence played a part in my ability to see myself as a leader. I also learned about how my upbringing and observations of my influencers made me believe certain things about myself, relationships in my life, and the world around me.

I also learned about the three different ways to exercise power through influence over others: through logical, emotional, and cooperative appeals.

It was also clear that in some situations, it's hard to know which of these things you are in tune with. Does anyone else ask, "Am I being logical enough in this situation? Am I sounding confident enough? Am I competent enough?" I often wondered about these things in hindsight, but while in the moment, it's hard to see how one is coming across.

AN ENTREPRENEURIAL MINDSET IN LEADERSHIP

According to the Merriam-Webster dictionary, an entrepreneur is "one who organizes, manages, and assumes the risks of a business or enterprise."[33] It seems straight-forward enough. I wanted to see some examples of how this word is used by the masses, so I typed it into the Urban Dictionary.

Some of the definitions that showed up made me chuckle. You should try looking up entrepreneur on Urban Dictionary someday. The term entrepreneur appears to be used as a catch-all for many things nowadays. In some circles, it seems that you cannot call yourself an entrepreneur unless you're working in technology or something glitzy or glamorous, or something brand new. I know entrepreneurs who have been working on the same business, growing it, and eventually selling it after thirty years.

However, that's not entirely the definition I'm referring to. What do I mean by entrepreneurial leadership? For one thing, being an entrepreneur does not automatically make one a leader; nonetheless, it gives you good context for what I mean by entrepreneurial leader.

Imagine, if you will, that the "leader" version of you is the product you're taking to market.

---

33 *Merriam-Webster*, s.v. "entrepreneur (_n._)," accessed July 26, 2020.

Also imagine that you need to do enough research on the product itself, sort of as an inventory or assessment of the current state of things.

How would you start? Well, for one thing, you would look at other leaders in the marketplace, particularly in your industry. You may even want to learn from their thought leadership (I'm thinking of the likes of Gary Vaynerchuk. He has an amazing following where he shares some simple, yet effective, advice on how to be an effective leader and entrepreneur.)

You can also go and follow every single group on social media that shares inspirational leadership quotes.

However, just looking at other leaders and potentially trying to mimic their styles won't be *your* unique value proposition to the market. While being an entrepreneur, you should be learning about your industry, your customer segments and using an iterative process to come up with the minimum viable product (MVP) that you take to market. The leader version of you must take a similar approach. Many people assume that if they have developed a product or service that they are automatically a leader. The version of *you* that you take to market as a leader must be the result of a thorough self-discovery process, that you will iterate over time. It cannot simply be repackaging the way others lead and rebranded as your own style. Perhaps that's how leaders start off, but that approach will have to evolve for that individual over time. The last thing you want is for people to see you as not being a genuine leader. If a brand cannot survive in today's marketplace without authenticity, neither can your personal leadership brand. The same rules apply as if the leadership version of you was a start-up.

REDISCOVERING THE LEADERSHIP VERSION OF YOU

We can't really use a startup mentality for a new company because you're not a new person. You're not a brand-new baby coming out of the womb. You've been around, you have baggage from your childhood, and you have emotional baggage from the workplace, your school, etc.

People have led you your whole life, though, and you may have a good sense of the leaders you liked and the ones you didn't like. It's not enough to simply go get an MBA or some other graduate degree, go look at some other leaders, and, POOF, you're a leader. You must take a true assessment of who you are, which includes taking inventory of who you are as a leader. And if you've been led enough times, so you have enough data points to understand what type of leader you want to emulate.

What does that mean though? A big part of this is taking stock of all the people who led you, the good, the bad, and the ugly. This is different from double-clicking on inspirational quotes that make you feel motivated on Instagram. These are examples of people who you directly reported to or even people who reported to you. Clearly, with family, there is a certain pecking order in most households with parents sitting at the top. A spreadsheet may or may not be a critical part of this assessment. It's entirely up to you.

I know tons of tests do this more in depth, and I would recommend that everybody do those as well. The more you can learn, the better. It's taking a slightly different approach in that in your own mind you're naming names. You're confronting your leadership demons.

It's more of a reflective process, not just looking at your own leadership skills and follies but looking at where those skills and follies came from. It's looking at the village of leaders that made you who you are today. It's not meant to be a complicated, scientific test. It's simply an organized way to reflect on yourself.

THE IN POWER TO EMPOWER SELF-ASSESSMENT

Make a list of all the people who you would consider a leader in your life, even if they aren't an authority figure. This can be a family member, a teacher, a friend, somebody from the media, a real or fictitious character from a book or movie. It could be anybody who once led or influenced you.

Try to list at least two to three for each of your major age buckets (age ranges listed below). You should have a total of at least ten people with no maximum (however, I'd suggest capping it at fifteen or twenty so you can move forward from reflecting and don't get stuck in analysis paralysis mode):

Childhood Years (Birth through pre-teen years)

	A family member	A friend	An authority figure	A real person from the media	A fictitious character from a book or movie	Other
Childhood years (Birth through pre-teen years)						
What are some descriptive words to describe their leadership style?						
What are some of the pros and cons of their style?						
Rate the effectiveness of their leadership style from 1 to 5, 1 for least effective and 5 for more effective						
How did this person's leadership style make you feel a majority of the time? 1 for bad, 5 for good						

Would you want this person to lead you in any part of your life right now, personally or professionally? 1 for no 5 for yes				
Does this person still impact how you make decisions about yourself or others? 1 for low impact, 5 for high impact				
Add a score of 1 in this row if you recall this person utilizing logical appeals				
Add a score of 1 in this row if you recall this person utilizing emotional appeals				
Add a score of 1 in this row if you recall this person utilizing cooperative appeals				

Formative Years (Teen years through twenty-one years old)

	A family member	A friend	An authority figure	A real person from the media	A fictitious character from a book or movie	Other
Formative years (Teen years through 21-years old)						
What are some descriptive words to describe their leadership style?						
What are some of the pros and cons of their style?						
Rate the effectiveness of their leadership style from 1 to 5, 1 for least effective and 5 for more effective						
How did this person's leadership style make you feel a majority of the time? 1 for bad, 5 for good						

Would you want this person to lead you in any part of your life right now, personally or professionally? 1 for no 5 for yes				
Does this person still impact how you make decisions about yourself or others? 1 for low impact, 5 for high impact				
Add a score of 1 in this row if you recall this person utilizing logical appeals				
Add a score of 1 in this row if you recall this person utilizing emotional appeals				
Add a score of 1 in this row if you recall this person utilizing cooperative appeals				

Early Adulthood (Twenty-one years old through thirty years old)

	A family member	A friend	An authority figure	A real person from the media	A fictitious character from a book or movie	Other
Early adulthood (21-years old through 30-years old)						
What are some descriptive words to describe their leadership style?						
What are some of the pros and cons of their style?						
Rate the effectiveness of their leadership style from 1 to 5, 1 for least effective and 5 for more effective						
How did this person's leadership style make you feel a majority of the time? 1 for bad, 5 for good						

Would you want this person to lead you in any part of your life right now, personally or professionally? 1 for no, 5 for yes				
Does this person still impact how you make decisions about yourself or others? 1 for low impact, 5 for high impact				
Add a score of 1 in this row if you recall this person utilizing logical appeals				
Add a score of 1 in this row if you recall this person utilizing emotional appeals				
Add a score of 1 in this row if you recall this person utilizing cooperative appeals				

Mature Adulthood (Thirty-one years old through forty years old)

	A family member	A friend	An authority figure	A real person from the media	A fictitious character from a book or movie	Other
Mature adulthood (31-years old through 40-years old)						
What are some descriptive words to describe their leadership style?						
What are some of the pros and cons of their style?						
Rate the effectiveness of their leadership style from 1 to 5, 1 for least effective and 5 for more effective						
How did this person's leadership style make you feel a majority of the time? 1 for bad, 5 for good						

Would you want this person to lead you in any part of your life right now, personally or professionally? 1 for no 5 for yes				
Does this person still impact how you make decisions about yourself or others? 1 for low impact, 5 for high impact				
Add a score of 1 in this row if you recall this person utilizing logical appeals				
Add a score of 1 in this row if you recall this person utilizing emotional appeals				
Add a score of 1 in this row if you recall this person utilizing cooperative appeals				

Wiser Adulthood (Forty-one years and above)

	A family member	A friend	An authority figure	A real person from the media	A fictitious character from a book or movie	Other
Wiser Adulthood (41-years old and above)						
What are some descriptive words to describe their leadership style?						
What are some of the pros and cons of their style?						
Rate the effectiveness of their leadership style from 1 to 5, 1 for least effective and 5 for more effective						
How did this person's leadership style make you feel a majority of the time? 1 for bad, 5 for good						

Would you want this person to lead you in any part of your life right now, personally or professionally? 1 for no 5 for yes					
Does this person still impact how you make decisions about yourself or others? 1 for low impact, 5 for high impact					
Add a score of 1 in this row if you recall this person utilizing logical appeals					
Add a score of 1 in this row if you recall this person utilizing emotional appeals					
Add a score of 1 in this row if you recall this person utilizing cooperative appeals					

If you're wondering why you have to work when you're just trying to read a book and magically snap your fingers and become a great leader, then we already have a long way to go. Great leaders have to do a lot of homework and self-reflection.

After filling in the charts, ask yourself the following questions about each person:

- **Leadership Style Score**
  - **What is their leadership style?** You don't have to look up any social science terms for this. Simply drop some descriptive words here. Believe me, especially if you're a seventies, eighties, or nineties baby, your parents were not reading books on how to lead you ;).
  - **What are some of the pros and cons of their style?** Again, no need to use psychological terms here, just some memories of what you liked or disliked.
  - **How effective was this leadership style?** While this person was leading you, did they convince you to comply with their requests? No need for an essay here, but let's add a rating here: 1 for least effective and 5 for most effective.
  - **How did this person's leadership style make you feel most of the time?** 1 for bad, 5 for good.
  - **Would you want this person to lead you in any part of your life right now, personally or professionally?** 1 for no, 5 for yes.
  - **Does this person still impact how you make decisions about yourself or others?** 1 for low impact, 5 for high impact.
- Tally those up ^^

- Influence Appeal Score
  - Then separately, also indicate which type of tactics each person employed by giving a score of 1 for each of the following types of influencing tactics (using definitions from the Center for Creative Leadership):
    - **Logical influencing tactics** (the Head) address people in a rational or intellectual way. Arguments and information such as facts and figures are brought forward in the best interest of the organization, the team, or the person.
    - **Emotional influencing tactics** (the Heart) connect the communication or decision to a person's feelings of well-being or sense of belonging. The leader appeals to attitudes, values, a common purpose, ideals, and beliefs through inspiration or enthusiasm.
    - **Cooperative influencing tactics** (the Hands) involve seeking advice and offering assistance. The leader reinforces the connection that he or she has with the others. Collaborating to accomplish a mutually important goal extends a hand to others.

Here are my hypotheses:
- **High Logical Appeal:**
  - A lower leadership style score with a majority logical appeal indicates that you generally use less emotion and pure metrics to lead both yourself and others. And when you don't meet those metrics, you consider yourself a failure. But that's similarly how you also treat other people. You may also lean more toward a fixed mindset.

- A higher leadership style score here with a majority logical appeal implies that, while logic and metrics are utilized to measure yourself and others, you have generally experienced and exercised flexibility to allow for growth and adjustment. You may lean more toward a growth mindset.

- **High Emotional Appeal:**
  - A lower leadership style score with a majority emotional appeal implies that you are leading both yourself and others using negative emotions such as fear and shame. You find that these are tactics are effective, at least in the short-term, but you may not be satisfied with your long-term results managing people and relationships in your life. Most of your engagements where you may have to deliver or receive bad news or provide or receive feedback are negative or confrontational. You may also lean more toward a fixed mindset.
  - A higher leadership style score with a majority emotional appeal might mean that you lead with a high emotional intelligence quotient. You are effective in your use of emotions when appealing to people. But sometimes, this might run out if you are leading or reporting to people who respond better to measuring success tangibly. So, you might be effective in appealing to people's emotions, but you might not necessarily be able to use this appeal long term in your career because at some point you must be measured based on logical or numerical values or metrics.

- **High Cooperative Appeal:**
  - A lower leadership style score with a majority cooperative score may be less likely to be the case unless you

manage to terrorize people en masse. Just kidding, but in reality, if you have a lower leadership style score, you may be less likely to appeal to multiple people at the same time to work together to solve problems or complete tasks.

- However, if you have a high leadership style score with a majority cooperative score, then your strong suit or your ability to lead comes from your wanting to work and problem-solve in a group setting. And you might also like to lead others to do the same.

I might check off some other areas too, but I think my leadership style is probably highly cooperative. I love working within teams. I love being an equal member of a team, so I don't necessarily care if I'm leading the team, but I like working together with a team to solve a problem. I like to feel equal in terms of team value or leadership value, but I like working with people with different expertise levels to solve a problem.

Similarly, I like to lead clients to work in that way as well. I like running workshops and bringing people together. And I like directing the room on how they can solve a problem together. I am a team player, but at the same time, I thrive in those environments. I like riffing off of people. I also think a cooperative style is an effective tool in making big decisions with all the right people in the room at the same time.

For example, when you're working on a big proposal for a client, many people nowadays might just say let's just email each other back and forth one thousand times, or let's just message each other on our communications channel until our fingers fall off. In reality, those are the times when people need to get on the phone or meet in person and talk it out.

There's a time and a place for every type of appeal. As a good leader, you need to see when to use which style. This assessment gives you a baseline for where you are coming from. So, if I looked at myself five years ago, or even ten years ago, I would probably say that working in a cooperative setting was probably not my strong suit because I always felt like my voice was never heard. But this stems from me coming from an environment where even though I spoke, I felt like I wasn't heard or my opinion didn't matter—not just as a leader, but as a follower.

I didn't care for those types of environments. I relied on work I did by myself to shine. Everyone was competing for the leader's attention, and I felt like I would get drowned out by other people. I led heavily with emotions before; that was my baseline and still comes most naturally to me now. And I use that a lot in my early career. In hindsight, it appeared that I could not use logical appeals as much because I did not feel confident in myself due to a lack of experience or knowledge. Slowly, though, my appeals have evolved over time.

Present day, I would say that I utilize cooperative appeals when appropriate. maybe I'm a great leader, and maybe I'm not. But I do feel like I can direct large groups of people at once to complete a task or objective. I can effectively communicate my vision and make sure that most of the people in a group understand my vision. That is my preferred style and where I am the strongest. So that's my assessment.

NOW WHAT?

This assessment is a way to level set the reader's individual leadership and appeal style, so if you feel like you're more logical and you're not finding success the way you like, then maybe you need to explore some ways to incorporate emotional appeals into your leadership style. I'm trying to turn it into a formula for people who need a formula. This is a directional, not scientific, baseline. Before you apply to a graduate program to become a leader or put money down the drain to learn more hard skills, stop and identify your gap.

For example, if you have a high analytical background and you think getting a graduate degree or certificate in a highly analytical field will make you a leader, where you can lead large groups of people, don't fool yourself. If you already have a logical background, you need to learn more of a soft skill if the next step you want to take in your career is leading humans. If you have a highly technical background, then getting a PhD in a technological field won't teach you how to lead people. Yes, if that area interests you, then certainly go and learn and get that higher degree. That is a recipe for being a thought leader on a particular topic or can even get you a teaching gig. It won't teach you how to teach, though.

If your objective is to be a leader of people, a leader of human beings, not just thought, you should be taking a different route. I won't tell you what route that is, but at a bare minimum, you should know your starting point and what you are going into the market with so that you can evolve and iterate just like a startup would. You should know your most valuable quality and take that leadership skill to market. Then evolve or iterate upon yourself from there.

That might beg the question then: which side of you do you want to evolve? If you're a technologist, it might mean you've gotten very good at an application of a particular type of technology. If you want to move into management, would it be more beneficial for your evolvement as a leader to learn seven more types of technology? You could be a technology professional and be leading teams with fear or shame, which are emotional appeals. "If you don't meet this deadline, you're going to get fired." Or "if you don't finish this on time, this project is going to fail and it will be all your fault." Just because you're a technical person does not mean you are using logic to lead.

It's important to understand your starting point because then you know which area you need to develop more. **You must anchor everything you do in what you know to be the truth about yourself, your abilities, your weaknesses, and areas of improvement.** There's no way to see the future unless you acknowledge your present and your past. This is also helping you lay the foundations for what many bloggers and life coaches like to call "self-awareness."

Now, you're ready to rock and roll.

PART TWO

PRINCIPLES OF ENTREPRENEURIAL LEADERSHIP

Now that we've determined our baselines, we are now ready to learn about Principles of Entrepreneurial Leadership.

You'll either lead or be led. If you don't like how you're being led, then you'll either cry about it, write songs or books about it, or do something even more drastic in order to overthrow power and/or obtain power for yourself. A smart leader identifies the opposition leader and works on either forming an alliance with them or eliminating them. Either that or maybe I've read one too many history books or watched one too many Marvel movies; however, there are many lessons about leadership in them.

Most people tend to focus on the external factors or conditions that surround those who lead and those who are led. But it is equally, if not more, important to look inside of yourself.

- Are you the leader or are you the one being led? In most corporate cultures, one could say both.
- What makes you believe that you are a leader?
- If you are a leader, then are you a successful leader? How are you measuring success?
- Do others agree with your measures?
- If you're not yet a leader, or at least don't believe you are yet, then how do you plan on getting there?

So many of us are in situations every day where we have to inspire or direct a group of people to achieve a desired outcome. Being a leader can mean using specific self-management tactics and self-discipline to complete a task or set of tasks to a desired outcome. It can also mean managing others to complete tasks or a set of tasks, as well as inspiring those who manage others who complete tasks.

If the tasks are completed for naught or the project is a bust or a company shuts down, will your companions or colleagues still consider you a leader?

That's exactly what you still are—a leader. When people respect you and want to take direction from you even when you've made mistakes before, that is a true sign of being a leader. They are not obligated to follow you but consider it a privilege because they believe in the same values as you. They may question you, and be truthful with you about their doubts, but they will give you a chance to explain what you envision.

Wouldn't that be the perfect world where you didn't have to constantly communicate your vision to people completely different from you? Leadership, good leadership at least, is not as easy as that.

But what makes a good leader?

- Business acumen
- Experience
- Technical knowledge
- Authenticity
- Credentials (MBA, PhD, certifications, etc.)
- Soft skills

What the heck does "soft skills" mean? Sure, you can read all the books and blogs teaching you about these, but how do you use your soft skills in real life? And when?

We will explore that during this part of the book and how these soft skills can become your [super] power.

WHAT WILL THIS SECTION COVER?

This section will walk through what I believe are the principles of entrepreneurial leadership:

- **Start by looking at yourself.** We started this process by establishing our baseline in the previous section.
- **Develop the right mindset.** Sometimes we have to shed our limitations in a wholesale fashion.
- **Take a new look at power.** It's not the damning force you might have believed it to be. And it may not come from the same source as it historically may have for others.
- **Be *the* people person.** Your team, your company, or any other group you are trying to lead really won't exist without people. They should be able to trust you.
- **Be strategic.** Being a leader means solving problems while seeing the big picture and understanding the tactical implications.
- **Disrupt where needed.** You don't have to be a disruptor every time, everywhere you go. There is a time and a place; use your judgment wisely.

CHAPTER 5

ANCHOR YOURSELF IN YOUR OWN TRUTH

———

One of the hardest parts of feeling like a leader is getting rid of all those nagging doubts about yourself from your head. You can avoid hearing actual humans by not being around them anymore, but how do you get rid of the thoughts in your head.

First, you must believe the opposite of the doubts you have about yourself. Only you should be telling the story of your personal brand; you get to tell it, not your titles or your heritage. Those are a part of you. They do not have to define you.

UNDOING FEELING LIKE A POSER

When I started working at Accenture's Innovation Center, I suffered from severe imposter syndrome. Every single day, I was so afraid somebody would figure out I wasn't one of them. I did not start at Accenture early on in my career like most people around me. I came in the middle of a career, but not necessarily as a manager or a subject-matter expert. I had a lot of self-doubt, and I didn't know if I was doing the right thing for my career or for my self-confidence at that point.

A lot of my friends were super impressed that I was working at Accenture, but I didn't really talk about it much at the time. In hindsight, I learned so much from that experience. I had a chance to sit in rooms with C-suite executives from Fortune 500 companies across different industries, while they made some of the biggest decisions in their company for the next five years. And the funny thing is, I didn't think I was good enough to be in those board rooms with them.

The clients in the room were probably twenty-five to thirty years older than me, and I was their target market. A couple of my managers at Accenture, who were both intelligent, strong, women (Karen Voelker, Global Retail Lead of Innovation and Allison Hofferica, Accenture Customer Innovation Center Lead at the time) would actually tell me, "Hey Afroze, if you have an idea, you should speak up because you probably have a different way of looking at the world than the clients do. They'll appreciate it." I eventually garnered up the courage to speak up in those rooms, and I am so glad they encouraged me to do so.

I am right on the cusp of people who first got internet during my early teen years. (Thank you, Mom and Dad, for getting that PC computer that took up an entire eighth of the room back then. And for the dial-up internet. I will never forget that sound.) Five to ten years ago, the C-suite at major corporations were *so* disconnected from this demographic.

But there I was, right in the room, able to tell them how I no longer went to the grocery store and how I ordered my groceries online, and how I took Uber and Lyft everywhere. People in the room had access to personal assistants and black car services. They found it interesting that this broke graduate student had the same luxuries in life at a fraction of the cost.

The discovery many times was, "We have an entire department of people just like her in our marketing and social media department who we should be listening to more," or, "We should be talking to the interns and listening to their ideas more. Our customers are less like us and more like them."

Toward the end of my time there, I started sharing in workshops that I was a graduate student. I did not realize how much people in the C-suite actually **wanted to know** what I thought. I was also in the right environment where the clients were clearly in that space to grow, learn, and innovate.

You must believe that you can add value everywhere you go. When you believe, you will start doing it.

OWNING YOUR HERITAGE

As much as this is about rejecting what you don't want; a lot of it is about deciding what you want to keep and own.

I'm not saying it's easy, but a big part of who I am is where I came from and where my family came from. I have a love-hate relationship with my culture. Some days, I'm boppin' to all my golden-oldie Bollywood jams, and other days, I'm venting on my blog about how much I hate people who look like me because of their incessant need to judge each other.

People who are not a part of a minority ethnic group might not understand that Asian immigrant communities become part of the village that raises you, even here in the United States or Canada. And no, not every Indian person knows each other. There are little pockets across the country, usually in religious communities (Hindu, Muslim, Sikh, Christian).

There's also a cross-country network that might be based on people being from the same village back in India or being a part of the same religious community but in a different city. The identity struggle happens when you can no longer find things to relate with in those communities (other than maybe the other people your age/generation going through the same thing as you).

So, while people like me are going through so much personal and professional growth, you encounter people in the community who potentially have the same measuring stick from ten to fifteen years ago. You realize it doesn't just apply to you anymore. You miss having the community in your life, but you choose to reject it.

But my culture isn't going anywhere. I'll always look like this, so either I'll be a part of the problem by judging the people who are judging me, or I'll teach people how to get out of their rut. Heck, even I've judged people (I judge people who fully reject their culture, their language, their food, and their people), but I'm trying to be more empathetic because I can truly understand the struggle within. People who want to grow and change will do so.

Having learned multiple languages as a child has helped my brain to develop. My husband and I plan to teach our future child to speak all the languages that we speak. We can communicate in six languages between the two of us but speak in English, Gujarati, and Urdu fluently with each other. I'm learning French and Swahili, which he speaks fluently, and he's learning Spanish, which I can speak well.

And research supports the idea of embracing your multilingual brain. "In the past, bilinguals were looked down upon," said Judith F. Kroll, Distinguished Professor of Psychology, Linguistics, and Women's Studies at Penn State University. "Not only is bilingualism not bad for you, it may be really good. When you're switching languages all the time, it strengthens your mental muscle and your executive function becomes enhanced."[34]

GET YOUR MENTAL HEALTH IN ORDER

No one should have to pay for your emotional baggage, especially not the people you are trying to lead. I wanted to touch upon this because it's such a big part of all the growth I have experienced in the past few years.

A licensed professional can play a big part in rediscovering yourself in a new light. They can help you look closely at your

---

[34] Victoria M. Indivero, "Think Twice, Speak Once: Bilinguals Process Both Languages," Penn State University, September 10, 2013.

formative years because they are just that: formative. Here are some themes I started to notice in myself because of this type of rediscovery:

- Siblings: not sure if I can say this because I am an only child, but that may be why I can say this. People who belong to a set of siblings have all sorts of strange complexes. My parents each have siblings; my husband has siblings; many of my friends have siblings. Here are some things I have observed:
  - They have a good relationship when there is a good balance of power, and they respect each other.
  - They have a bad relationship when there is an imbalance or perceived imbalance of power (superiority/inferiority complexes).
  - Because I was an only child, I'm always looking for the camaraderie I've seen others in my life experience by having a sibling. I have had close friends and other family members fill that void, but I will always feel it, no matter what I try to do.
- Parents: There was a definite power struggle between parents. I observed it, I heard it, and I understood it. I did not fully understand why, but I knew it was there.
  - This is different from the power struggle I saw between my parents as spouses to each other.
  - I learned this from friends who had siblings and those times when I went to a co-ed school: a gender power imbalance existed among children when I was growing up. I don't know if it's the same now for children, but it was the case for me.

- Many households, including mine, used emotion as a means to an end. Also, new, modern parenting styles address relying on the emotional appeal far too much.
- These emotional methods still work on me sometimes, especially when coming from my parents. The seeds were planted in my younger days. I have been using their effects to work toward being a happier version of myself.
- I could on go and on, but you get the point.

When you are self-aware, you can look at all the things you learned during your formative years (and beyond) to decide what about your behavior you want to keep, refine, or get rid of. Here's my summary:

- My mom tends to listen a lot and not speak up too often. I might not agree with this tactic for all situations, but I find it useful many times. When I am with clients or in a situation that requires someone to be heard, I actively listen more first before responding. Am I perfect at this? No, but it's a work in progress like so many other things.
- My dad tends to be particularly...persistent until he gets what he wants. I think many people might be able to say that about their parents. It's not my favorite quality, but it's effective. I like to use this tactic carefully and only as a last resort. My first assumption is that the person on the receiving end of my request will complete the ask in a reasonable and timely fashion. When they do not complete an ask, I feel OK believing that they are simply busy.

BE HAPPY, BE JOYFUL

Therapy, self-care, taking breaks when you need them, having alone time, going on a trip to awaken your spirit, drinking another cup of coffee because you just wanted to, staying up late to watch your favorite TV shows—the list can go on and on.

Stop depriving yourself of joy. It's your responsibility as a future leader to learn how to be joyful so you can teach others the same thing. Being a leader is an incredible responsibility. I see this all the time among people on the same team.

Two teammates, one admires the other and they're both about the same age. One works frantically about sixteen hours a day on their day job and side projects because that's just who he is. He's been doing it for a while so he can get through his day job tasks quickly and do things thoroughly. The other person is new at it, so she tries to get through it quickly but does not do a quality job. Stop mimicking what others are doing and find the rhythm for what is good for you.

Why is all this important? How can you convince someone that you can lead them if you cannot face your own demons?

- Get ahead of the things about you that you don't understand, or dislike.
- Own the parts of yourself that are a part of your truth, no matter how much others try to convince you of your wrongness.

- You are responsible for your own happiness. But when you lead, you are also responsible for leading by example and allowing others to be happy too. They are entitled to happiness as human being, and so are you. So be happy. Be joyful.

CHAPTER 6

MINDSET IS 75 PERCENT OF THE BATTLE

———

An important shift in my career in the past ten years is that I know how limited my thinking was before and how differently I can think now. This is critical for me to be able to solve complex problems for clients and even for myself.

I suggest determining what type of mindset you have and developing the right mindset if you haven't already. I had people telling me this all the time. It's much harder to wrap your head around it and apply it to yourself until you go through the transformation yourself.

Early on in my career, I would often respond to advice or feedback from my teammates, friends, or superiors with emotion. I would either feel ashamed that I didn't already know what people were telling me about myself or I would feel angry at others' audacity for telling me something I already knew. Additionally, it felt frightening that the limited knowledge I had at twenty-one or twenty-four or twenty-six was all I would ever know for the rest of my life. It probably felt that way because I was not receptive to new information or knowledge.

Here's the thing: many of us know a lot of things. We've learned by reading things and watching each other, but do we always apply what we know to real-life situations? When initially learning things, we might find them very relevant to our general knowledge bank, but we might not be able to recall the information when presented with a situation. Aside from being self-aware, the only other way to know whether you are effectively doing your job or communicating your thoughts is to get feedback. How I received feedback told me that I was not open to growing.

GROWTH MINDSET VS. FIXED MINDSET

I did not realize there was a concept to describe these different kinds of mindsets until I was in graduate school at Northwestern University's Medill School of Journalism, Media, and Integrated Marketing Communications. I took an elective class at Northwestern's business school (Kellogg School of Management) called **Entrepreneurship: Building Innovation, Teams, and Cultures**. The class was about building innovation teams and cultures at start-ups and mature organizations. That's where Professor Joe Dwyer introduced me (and the rest of our class) to the idea of growth versus fixed mindset. I still did not know what that meant in practice, but I knew I had a lot of shifting to do in my own mindset.

According to Carol S. Dweck, author of *Mindset: The New Psychology of Success*, and a highly revered expert in the fields of personality, social psychology, and developmental psychology, there are two very distinct mindsets: growth mindset and fixed mindset. Carol Dweck's framework for growth vs fixed mindset is based on how individuals approach challenges, obstacles, effort, criticism, and the success of others. I like this framework because these are some of the moments in an individual's life and career where your knowledge, patience and pride are all tested. I still have a long way to go when it comes to having a growth mindset but knowing that I am aiming to have a growth mindset guides my actions and helps me to reflect on my actions when they do not reflect a growth mindset.[35]

What is fixed mindset and what is growth mindset?

Someone with a **fixed mindset** believes that they already know everything they are ever meant to know and are very concerned with appearing smart, even if they might not be. They believe it's enough to be talented and effort should not be required to obtain success. They may ignore feedback and avoid large amounts of effort if they feel like they can find a shortcut or a faster more efficient way to do everything. In the long run, according to Dweck, they may plateau early and achieve less than what they have the potential to achieve.[36]

Someone with a **growth mindset**, on the other hand, feels that whatever they know now is a point in time in their knowledge base. They are eager to learn things all the time and, as a result, are in a better position to solve problems,

---

35   Carol Dweck, *Mindset*: The New Psychology of Success (New York: Penguin House, 2016), 6, 7.
36   Dweck, *Mindset*, 3-14.

and bring new perspectives to problems that might have been supposedly solved before. They are open to new information and are more likely to obtain long-term success, even if, in the short-term, they may not appear to be the smartest or most successful person in the room. They view effort as a means to acquiring competence in a particular area, as opposed to "work". They learn from the criticism received and find inspiration from the success of others. In the long run, they have a better chance of achieving more success and more sustained success.[37]

When I started graduate school, I had been working at Accenture's Innovation Center for about one year, and I could not understand why it seemed like some people who came through the center, "got it" and why others seemed like they didn't "get it." I spent a lot of time observing people's reactions to new information and ideas during those workshops.

These workshops usually had people from all functions of an organization that ranged from C-suite to senior leadership teams to upper and middle management. Organizational dynamics and politics were in full effect during many of the discussions. Most of the individuals who attended these sessions were change agents and were open to hearing things that could not only help them do their jobs better but also aid the company in either becoming more efficient or finding new revenue opportunities. However, some individuals attended these sessions with myopic views of what they needed to solve for and did not feel like

---

37   Dweck, Mindset, 15-16.

they needed to learn something new. The amazing workshop facilitators and subject-matter experts did a great job guiding the groups through productive discussions and ideation sessions.

I took everything I learned and watched it in action every day at work. While I can benefit from learning until my last breath, during this time, I could feel my mindset shifting. It felt like an out of body experience where things suddenly started making sense. Understanding people, especially in organizations, planted the seeds for my career of being a strategist further down the road.

WHEN I GROW UP...
I observed my parents and many others from my formative years, especially how they fared in terms of their mindset. I had to reject their mindsets (which were more fixed than growth) in order to "break the mold." If I had to draw a direct line from decisions I've made back to the people who influenced those decisions, where would those lines end up?

Early on in life, I could probably draw many of those lines back to my parents and our religious community. These influenced much of my behavior and what I considered acceptable versus unacceptable.

Over time, those lines went as far out as my friends, my teachers, my colleagues and bosses, and even people on television and in the movies. If you're not actively seeking out others who will help shape your mindset, then you will continue to have the same types of outcomes.

For example, I grew up around many adults who believed in superstitions or luck. I do not want to confuse this with organized religion but simply myths of having bad luck or good luck because you did or didn't do something right. I prefer to respect how people explain that which cannot be explained, but that did not mean I also had to believe that myself.

One person in particular, let's call him Mr. Ned Negatively, constantly repeated how he had the worst luck in the world. He would only see his luck when things went badly for him. Whenever things went well, he would wait for the other shoe to drop. He could not see the positive in his life, and he would start most conversations with, "The problem is..." or "I'm worried about..."

When it came to looking outside of himself, Ned would only see the bad in the world. "Look at how much crime exists in the world. Look at all the religious conflicts. Look at all the corruption. It's all going downhill from here. Be careful, Afroze. You have to be prepared for this god-awful world that you'll encounter in the future."

It isn't like he was focusing on untruths. All those things contained truth: there was a lot of bad in the world. I started to see the world that way too, eventually. I felt depressed and helpless because I was only focusing on the problems and ruminating about the bad in the world.

But there was also a lot of good in the world. Each of those negative situations had a flip side. And those were the conversations I would try to have with him. While crime exists in the world, more people are good and kind, but we don't hear about it.

And there has been religious conflict in the world since there have been religions. The religions don't really cause the conflicts: it's the people who feel like there can't be differing views in the world *and* the politicians who use that to fuel their agenda for wealth, war, power, or land.

But what did Ned base his conclusions on? If he was drawing his conclusions based on what he saw in the media, then it's obvious why he would feel this way. However, he also only surrounded himself with other people who thought like him. His closest friends were his friends because they all enjoyed commiserating about the dilapidating world around them.

For example, it would be hard to ignore what has been happening in India with Prime Minister Narendra Modi. Perhaps by the time this book is published, there will be a mutually beneficial resolution to the immigration policies skewed against non-Hindus, and specifically skewed against Muslims. As a Muslim, this makes me pretty angry and would probably make Ned angry too.

People like Modi, and political parties like Bharatiya Janta, will continue to exist in India and elsewhere and continue to use Hindu Nationalism to divide the country. However, if we focus on the fact that just as many people, if not more, are protesting their message of hatred and divisiveness, we might have a foundation of hope to build our point of view around.

I recently read an article in the January 25-30th issue of *The Economist* that quoted some political scientist of Hindu descent, who chose to remain anonymous, as he claimed that "an awful lot of Hindus" hate Muslims. According to this professor, he'd equate "an awful lot" to about 40 percent. I guess that's pretty bad. Based on the last census conducted in India in 2011, of the 996 million Hindus in India...the 40 percent who hate Muslims are 398,400,000 Hindus. 60 percent still either don't know how they feel, don't care, or do *not* hate Muslims.[38]

What are some ways to think through this? Let's use the fixed and growth mindset lenses to look at the information provided.

Outlook 1: Even though the numbers seem positive, the reality seems bleak.
- Start with some information.
- Make a decision that could define a very limited view going forward.
- Limit the possibility of opening yourself up to new information because you've already decided your stance on it. This outlook would probably belong to someone with a fixed mindset.

Outlook 2: Reality seems bleak, but the numbers seem positive.
- Start with what the perceived situation appears to be.
- See how the new information impacts your stance on the topic.

---

38 "Narendra Modi's Sectarianism Is Eroding India's Secular Democracy," *Economist*, January 23, 2020, accessed July 26, 2020.

- Leave an opening for new information. This outlook is most likely to come from someone who has a growth mindset.

Outlook 3: The numbers prove that Hindus hate Muslims. Therefore, Muslims must hate Hindus too.

- Many people benefit from using information to create an agenda-filled narrative, such as politicians.
- The word *prove* is a red flag when assessing the statement versus the information provided. The numbers quoted do not provide any indication that *all* Hindus hate Muslims. It also provides insufficient data for why Muslims should hate Hindus too.
- These divisive tactics win elections but do nothing for building a unified/cohesive environment.
- There is no room for new information when making statements like this. It's a very distinct stance.

Outlook 4: Why do the Hindu Nationalists dislike Muslims so much? Where have we seen this before?

- In this outlook, we are not really taking a side. We are asking inquisitive questions. We are still learning.
- One set of information cannot be enough to create an educated stance on something so very complex. There is *so much* that even I admittedly don't know about this situation.
- With this, we are not trying to determine if what is happening is right or wrong. We are simply trying to understand the facts and take the side of the truth.
- When we do this, we can learn about both sides, develop empathy based on facts, and continue to walk through life (as a Muslim) without animosity for the approximately

nine hundred million Hindus in the world. However, this is not about religion or differences in belief. It is purely politics at play.

I could probably create plenty of scenarios for how to analyze the situation in India. I know what you're thinking: again with the religion and politics? It's not an obsession, I swear. Ok, maybe it is. But they're two of the most powerful forces in the universe. They influence how we view the world and how we approach problem solving and critical thinking. We cannot do either if we let others "solve" problems for us and give us the answer, which often happens with religion and politics. These are great topics to start exercising and identifying a growth mindset in yourself and those around you.

It's all about how you look at the information presented to you. Additionally, if you surround yourself with people who will look at the world the same way as you, then in order to conform, you will never have a reason to change.

You get to determine your mindset. Then, whichever situation you are in—home, work, community, or school—you will be inspired to create this type of environment. When you can't find it in one place, you will seek it elsewhere.

This scenario and these emotions are on the more extreme side. But what about other less polarizing situations? How does one have a growth mindset in other less severe circumstances?

I'VE BEEN WORKING ON THIS PRESENTATION, ALL THE LIVE-LONG DAY

PowerPoint presentations, ping-pong tables, processes, flow charts, productivity software, messaging platforms, and happy hours do *not* create a company culture. Having worked in consulting and visited many client offices, manufacturing facilities, customer service call centers, and design and innovation centers, I've observed many working environments.

Many in leadership want to instill a growth mindset in their employees. That is a great thing, of course, because everyone should want to keep learning and growing in how they view themselves and the world around them. So many things prior to our professional lives impact what type of mindset we have in the workplace.

Ultimately, how people treat each other and their expectations for what is acceptable or not is set by those who claim to be the leaders. It is upon them to promise and deliver an environment that ensures that everyone feels safe and supported enough to do their work and care for themselves and their own. That creates culture in workplaces, homes, communities, and schools. This is what your staff sees, your children, your students, and so on.

People create culture. Good leaders listen, then reinforce or redirect what the culture should be for the greater good. So while everyone in a company might not have a growth mindset, the leaders must have a growth mindset.

How can you start training yourself to have more of a growth mindset?

LOOK BEYOND YOUR TRAINING

I have worked on a number of start-up projects—some in a larger capacity, others in smaller capacities. One of these start-up colleagues was trying so hard to be an "entrepreneur," and she did everything she could do on her checklist. She read all the blogs, watched all the webinars, and asked partners at various venture capital firms to coach her and review her pitch.

She focused on mimicking entrepreneur culture to become an entrepreneur *instead of simply trying to solve a market problem and solve it well.*

She often asked my thoughts while I was working at the Accenture Innovation Center. So I would, of course, do some research on her idea and provide my thoughts. I suggested she look at B corporations to certify her company by a third party and stand out from the competition. This came up because part of their value proposition was that their product would be good for the environment and good for everyone.

Her response was, "What's a B corporation? That's not a legal entity like a C corporation. I did not learn about it in my MBA program, and so, therefore, it does not exist or is not legitimate. Also, it costs way too much to get a certification like this, and it might not be worth the investment."

Maybe she was right in her own respect, but to disregard it completely was a bit...short-sighted in my opinion.

This is a problem for anyone who uses their formal training as a crutch: graduate and undergraduate programs teaching only facts and knowledge. They may try to plant seeds for what is to come, but don't take what you learned in textbooks as truth. The sole purpose of getting an education is to learn how to think, how to solve problems, and how to be resourceful. Unless you are in a forward-looking program where your sole purpose is to learn how to think for the future, you are still learning from the past.

A growth mindset does not mean piling on to the mess of a human you might have become at a certain point in time. We are all a mess—some more, some less. A growth mindset is reflecting on where you might have unnecessarily held yourself or others back because of arbitrary limitations, and never letting these get in your way again.

Our goal for being good leaders is to be both competent and confident, feel secure in our attachment style, and embrace a growth mindset.

CHAPTER 7

[SUPER]POWER REDEFINED

———

My view on power has shifted significantly, over the years and especially in the process of writing this book. It got me asking myself questions like:

- Where does one find power?
- Is looking for power bad? Does it make one power hungry?
- What if someone is looking for power to simply feel empowered themselves?
- When does power start being detrimental to being a good leader?

REVERSING THE SOURCES OF POWER

In my mind, power only exists in relation to something else. For example, I can believe that I have power, but if I cannot accomplish anything with that power (empower myself, empower others, influence others, etc.), then do I really have power?

As we explored earlier, every leader in recorded history has gotten their power from somewhere. Something that they did or something that occurred convinced people that their leader has power (over them, over their resources, over their country, or over their company).

However, in this age of transparency and unconventional wisdom, people are more likely to want to *choose* who they allow to lead them. This is indicative of the rise of companies like Glassdoor, Indeed, and others where people can rate their former (or current) boss. It starts as early as college, when university students can rate their professors (http://ratemyprofessors.com). Uber customers can rate their drivers, and the drivers can rate their customers now, for Pete's sake. People don't just have the power through general representation; individuals have power collectively. When did we think that would happen?

Being a leader in this environment sounds like a serious feat. Leading in the present and into the future means being transparent, egalitarian, inclusive, and genuine. These can be best demonstrated by collaborating, communicating, and managing time and resources effectively.

Sounds pretty daunting, doesn't it? What does it mean in reality? Who has the power and who doesn't?

According to the US Census Bureau, jobs in the STEM workforce grew 79 percent from 1990 through 2016. This field is projected to grow 13 percent through 2027, compared to an average growth of other fields.[39] Of the over 1.4 million job openings, it is predicted that US universities can only fill 29 percent of those roles.[40] That does not account for graduates who are not from US universities, nor does it account for students who might not be STEM graduates.

But that's not the real deficit.

Google did a study of its employees a few years ago and discovered that, while conventional wisdom dictates that students need to master STEM subjects and learn to code because that's where the jobs are, there is a lot more to it than that.

In 2013, Google did an analysis of every single piece of data on their employees since 1998, when the company was incorporated. This analysis included hiring data, firing data, and performance evaluation data. This project was called Project Oxygen. "Project Oxygen shocked everyone by concluding that, among the eight most important qualities of Google's top employees, **STEM expertise comes in dead last**. The seven top characteristics of success at Google are all soft skills: being a good coach; communicating and listening well; possessing insights into others (including others different values and points of view); having empathy toward and being supportive of one's colleagues; being a good critical thinker

39   Emsi, "Emerging Jobs & Skills in STEM," Economic Modeling Specialists International, April 2017.

40   Kalil, Tom. Jahanian, Farnam. "Computer Science is for Everyone!" The White House President Barack Obama Archives, December 2013.

and problem solver; and being able to make connections across complex ideas."[41]

SOFT SKILLS ARE THE NEW [SUPER]POWER

Soft skills have traditionally been considered weaknesses in leaders. Ironically, women were known to harness these softer skills. But even women have a hard time using these soft skills because they've been encouraged to be "harder" and "stronger" in the workplace, like the male leaders that have come before them and around them.

Soft skills are very closely related to emotional intelligence. According to an *HBR* article by Daniel Goleman back in 1998 (wow, that's more than twenty years ago!) called "What Makes a Leader?" Goleman identifies five components of emotional intelligence at work, along with some definitions that will serve as themes throughout this book:[42]

- Self-awareness: the ability to recognize and understand your moods, emotions, and drives, as well as their effect on others
- Self-regulation: the ability to control or redirect disruptive impulses and moods; the propensity to suspend judgment, to think before acting

---

41 Valerie Strauss, "The Surprising Thing Google Learned about Its Employees — And What It Means for Today's Students," *The Washington Post*, Dec. 20, 2017.

42 Daniel Goleman, "What Makes A Leader?" in *HBR's 10 Must Reads On Leadership* (Boston: Harvard Business School Publishing, 2011), 6.

- Motivation: a passion to work for reasons that go beyond money or status; a propensity to pursue goals with energy and persistence
- Empathy: the ability to understand the emotional makeup of other people; skill in treating people according to their emotional reactions
- Social skill: proficiency in managing relationships and building networks; an ability to find common ground and build rapport

Power in the past was defined by how much wealth or political clout someone had. Today, soft skills are the new [super] power. While it is important to learn the hard skills to land your dream job, as we learned from Google, it will be critical to master the soft skills to grow in your career in the long term.

CHAPTER 8

PEOPLE, THEN PROCESSES AND TECHNOLOGY

———

Never in the history of mankind has it been easier to be a good leader. With the use of development best practices, productivity, and collaboration tools, very few reasons exist for why someone cannot be a good leader other than they don't know how to utilize these things to their advantage.

Having so many screens, and apps and clicks and beeps and dings that come with managing people, tasks, workflows, projects, etc. is challenging because people are sitting on the other side of the screen. Those people might be customers/clients, colleagues, and even family and friends. We are increasingly using technology to live our lives, do our work, and maintain our relationships. One principle is to anchor yourself in people as opposed to other factors when planning, managing, or communicating.

What does that mean? Let's dive in a little deeper.

PEOPLE-FOCUSED VS. TASK-FOCUSED

So much of trying to be both competent and confident depends on knowing what to do but also when to apply it. So much of this is further dependent upon people. There is a time and a place to be concerned about the top line and the bottom line. However, fixating on those items even when the solution to certain problems and situations remains in people can be detrimental to progress.

For example, when hiring managers or human resource professionals take a task-focused approach to hiring, they are looking to find a body that can complete specific tasks. Plenty of roles at an organization are mission critical and require talent that can do a few tasks well. People who have the specific skills to get the task done can be great at their job for years.

However, when hiring for management or leadership positions, you cannot look for the same thing. It seems obvious, but, algorithms be damned, some keywords just don't do justice to finding the right *people* to inspire, lead, and manage people. Management implies moving from managing a series of tasks to managing an individual or multiple individuals who are each managing their own tasks while achieving a higher goal.

When leading people as if they are tasks, you will rely heavily on logical and emotional appeals. Logical appeals would be things like providing deadlines, creating timelines, and developing project plans. Emotional appeals in this case would mean creating a sense of urgency about deadlines by pointing at timelines and project plans. Sometimes the emotions that arise are less so in the management but in those being managed. Feelings like anxiety, stress, and irritation can create some hostile environments.

All the things noted above are the right things to do when managing tasks in a project. However, these aren't the best things to solely rely on when managing people.

I know what you're thinking: I'm not a project manager... these things are their problems. Well, yes, that's their job description but everyone gets impacted. Anyone who's gotten their PMP (Project Management Professional) certification can attest to the fact that they learn about looking at projects/programs holistically. However, I don't know of any PMO (project management organization) that takes the time to set everyone up for success.

The cooperative appeal differentiates task managers from people and implies that people have opportunities to come together somehow to solve a problem. This can happen in several different ways, and I will share some more examples in this chapter.

EMPATHY + PEOPLE DEVELOPMENT

One of the hardest things to do as a people manager is to decide whether it's worth investing the time and effort to train and develop people. If an individual you're managing lacks a certain skill set, do you let them go or teach them how to do the job? This is not as simple as someone not knowing how to use a productivity tool.

As a manager of people and tasks, you will discover that everyone lacks something or wishes they were better at something. No one knows everything, but those worth investing time in are the ones who want to learn and develop themselves.

At one of the start-ups I worked on, Nushii, I was involved in everything from picking the color of the countertop to the content on the website to social media accounts, the menu design, and the selection of the point-of-sale system. Once the restaurant opened, I was also responsible for training and orientation to ensure that we had an inclusive and positive work environment.

At Nushii, I spent a lot of time developing people and their skills. I invested time not for myself or for our business but to help them develop skills they could use for the rest of their lives, even if they worked elsewhere. Some of these individuals still reach out to me many years later.

I shared with the trainees that every problem has a solution, so when things start to feel sticky, they should first try to tackle the problem as best they could. If they couldn't, they were welcome to ask us. Everything taught in training needed to be mastered, but they could ask us for help for anything outside of that. Tests were conducted to ensure that people understood how many ounces of fish and other ingredients were to be used in the making of the sushi burritos and bowls.

After about six months of being open, an employee called me. I was traveling for my day job, so I could not meet with her in person. She felt like she could come to me, despite the two other partners in the city, one of them being my husband, the Director of Operations. This woman called me in tears, saying that Aly, the Director of Ops, wanted to promote her to catering and offsite manager.

I said that was great and I was really happy for her. She was not as thrilled and she shared, confidentially, that she did not understand how to do basic math or convert measurements very easily. She knew she would be tested on these skills before the formal promotion.

First, I tried to comfort her and remind her that everything has a solution. I gave her some tips. I told her that first, measurements are all around her. For example, next time she got a bottle of juice or soda, she should pour it into a measuring cup to easily start to see how many ounces are in a cup. Then I advised her to use Google as a tool to search for conversions or conversion tables. Lastly, I texted her some Khan Academy videos on how to learn basic math.

I later found out that she watched those videos during her bus commute to and from work and brought questions to Aly to learn properly. She was eager to learn everything! Equipped with these, I told her to ask the store manager for a few demonstrations. I worked with the Director of Ops and the store manager remotely to come up with a learning plan for her.

Fast forward, this employee took her test and passed. She became the catering and off-site manager and got a raise. She was a single mom in her thirties with four children. No one had ever taken the time to teach her these skills. When this worked with her, we offered this type of training to others who were interested. Nine other employees took advantage of the training within a few months. They were able to help any shift manager with the catering tasks, which made us more efficient and increased output for catering and off-site significantly.

Two years later, that employee keeps in touch with us, even though we now live in a different city. When the business closed, we helped her and many other former employees get jobs at other restaurants in the neighborhood. We had even befriended the regional manager of Halal Guys and referred some great employees to them as well. All our promotions were from within, and our staff learned skills they could take with them everywhere they went.

The key lesson here is very simple. I could have taught this employee basic math skills myself. She would have felt more powerful because, as we have always known, knowledge is power. But her need was a little more than knowledge. She needed to learn how to be resourceful so that whenever she had a problem, she could learn on her own whenever possible and feel more confident about asking her bosses questions. Someday, I hope she is the boss and others can learn from her. The solution here was not for her to feel like she was in power over her skills or over other people; the solution was to empower her for a longer-term impact.

ELEVATING OTHERS IS THE LOGICAL ROUTE

So why not just hire someone who knows how to do all these things and plop her in the role? We also had some discussions around this option, and, as logical as it seems, it wouldn't solve the problem holistically.

Even she could not understand why she was being given the opportunity, but a few of us in leadership saw it clearly. She had built an excellent rapport with the other employees. She had children at home, and she had plenty of leadership skills that came from being a mother. Having the ability to mobilize the other employees to get things done was her true talent.

Another important thing to note is that many times, we see people with a certain skill set and want to dream their future up for them. That works to a certain extent for helping them make certain advances in their careers while they're in our employ. However, if we focus on developing the whole person, not just the "role" we are in need of, we are more likely to develop loyalty in that individual and their work product will also be higher quality. They will have bought into your dream and will do anything to support it because they know you would do the same for their dream.

This chapter was about people, then process, then technology. Figure out what the people need, and then build the process around them. The example I shared was of a smaller business. How does this apply to bigger businesses or even in other types of businesses?

I believe many people who have an entrepreneurial streak will read this book. I have worked on several start-ups and have met many entrepreneurs. In the early days, as a start-up founder tries to build their team, they'll convince the people they are recruiting that "this is the next big thing" and they're going to be a part of greatness. Those are all wonderful things to aspire to, but one important thing is often overlooked. What exactly is the start-up trying to solve and can I genuinely believe in this concept?

I know what you're thinking: that's obvious. However, many individuals I speak to, especially about their careers, are more than willing to take a pay cut and work all kinds of wonky hours just to get some experience working with a start-up. Sounds glamorous at the outset; heck, I've fallen for these same types of reasons to join a start-up.

Gary Vee, the media mogul, has stated this in various ways, and I'll say it here too. The founder of a company and those who follow on the team would be motivated by very different things. Even among co-founders who partner to bring a solution to the world might be doing it for different reasons. Many start-ups are run with a plethora of emotions: ego, ambition, vanity, altruism, a desire to feel like someone important, etc. Some motivations are noble while others are not.

A leader in a start-up environment needs to strike a balance between meeting the start-up's goals while also respecting individual motivations for why people are in it. Leaders, founders, CEO's, etc., must know that this endeavor is a point in time for others; they cannot expect others to make it their own unless they truly feel that way about the product/solution being brought to market.

DIVERSITY IS NOT AN OPTION; IT'S A NECESSITY

Democratizing the process to select the best candidate for a job is a better approach for staffing. This is true not just for credibility's sake but because it's smart business. Nepotism, the act of hiring someone simply because of a connection outside of the workplace can create an unhappy work environment for others on the team who might not have had the same privilege. Additionally, limiting one's view because of some specific keywords on an applicant's resume is not the right approach to finding the right people for your team. This can happen when human resource specialists or hiring managers have a lot of information to sift through. This is where the ability to read between the lines to look for other important characteristics becomes helpful.

I love those stories or movies where the superhero is actually just one part of a larger team (I would be lying if the superhero I was thinking of wasn't Captain America and the team the Avengers, but then again, who wouldn't think that?). Everyone has their own strengths and weaknesses, but when they come together, they are stronger than any single bad guy.

I remember reading a book when I was a child called *The Ear, The Eye, and the Arm* by Nancy Farmer. The name indicates it might have been a biology book, but it was science fiction. Three children were in trouble, and their parents hired three detectives to help find them. The children all had very distinct personalities and strengths. As a child, I could not remember why the author focused so much on each of the children's temperaments. It didn't seem relevant. I was a critical eight-year-old about what I was reading. The three detectives, The Ear, The Eye, and The Arm (that was the name of their detective agency) also had very distinct personalities and very obvious special powers—the ability to hear way more than the average human ears, ultra-powerful sight, and the ability to stretch oneself super-humanly.

Each person had just the right abilities to deal with different situations. That was meaningful to me. In certain cases, the sister might have been the right person but did the older brother (the obvious leader in this story) *let* her step in and help? And vice versa? Tapping into people's special skill sets was a part of that equation too. And leadership *knowing* the different capabilities that different people possess could impact how effectively they are included in problem solving.

I think diversity in skill and thought is an important thing to consider when building teams. The other thing that falls under diversity is when developing an employee's skills. I learned the word fungibility during one of my more recent entrepreneurial stints, which in this instance means anything capable of mutual substitution or interchangeable. That's the theory that everyone in a business/team should know how to do everything (or most things) to avoid slowing down operations if someone does not show up or leaves. I got it and it's a great concept, except when it's not. What happens when you have a lot of specialists (does one thing great) and not enough generalists (does many things well)? Do you train those who are already employed to be versatile or do you get more people to do additional tasks that require new skills?

The answer to this is a fluid one. You cannot always spend the time to develop people and their skills. You also cannot always hire new people to do new tasks. It's a balancing act that must be properly managed by a good leader.

That brings up another point. When setting expectations with people on your team, it's very easy to overlook needs that might arise spontaneously. The ability to communicate with diversely skilled team members is the difference between uniting your team successfully and creating chaos.

This reminds me of a scene from one of my favorite TV shows, *NCIS* (which stands for Naval Criminal Investigative Service). The lead character, Leroy Jethro Gibbs, is the ultimate leader— former Marine, all-for-one and one-for-all attitude, moves quickly, does not let DC bureaucracy get in the way of saving people or getting justice. It also helps that he is ruggedly handsome. However, when he knows he has a weakness, he calls in others who he *knows* are experts. He leans on the strengths of his team members. And while he may be the lead, he does not have an ego and can let others take lead through the course of the show.

In one instance, (Season 2, Episode 12 for those of you who are fans), he asks a member of his team, Tim McGee, to accompany him to help translate an interview. Gibbs was a technophobe, and the person who needed to be interviewed was a technologist. McGee was an MIT graduate, and clearly a technophile.

The relationship between these two characters was that of mutual respect. McGee looked up to Gibbs for his street smarts, his years of experience, and his infamous "gut," which most people would simply call intuition. Gibbs respected

McGee for his ability to learn new things very quickly, his ability to use his tech-savviness to solve problems, and his ability to go outside of his comfort zone, especially when it came to being an NCIS field agent. The most wonderful thing about their relationship was they asked each other for help (most of the time). While one was the boss, both were leaders.

There is a lot to unpack here about how this applies to the real world. One of the pitfalls of saying, "I have a technology company; I'm going to get someone who speaks tech to lead it" is that your company will have an entire set of other humans running the company whose language will not be spoken in the future vision of the company. Getting someone who knows how to mobilize a group of people or many groups of people in an organization will probably be a more sustainable approach to deciding on a company's leadership.

SPEAK ENGLISH, JAVASCRIPT, AND HUMAN

When leaders lose themselves in the glitziness of technology or automation tools to improve processes, they waste a lot of time RFPing themselves into a frenzy. An RFP is a "request for proposal" that clients often send out when shopping for a new vendor partner. Leaders do not all have to be experts on technology; they do, however, have to be experts on solving problems. And where should you start when solving those problems? In a company, big or small, focus on the solutions, not the technology or the tools. Start with the people.

Without people, there are no companies and no need for technology or automation. Leaders of the past, present, and future all need to be able to speak human. Solve problems to what end you ask? **Create and improve processes utilizing platforms or technologies that are not cost-prohibitive to create a seamless experience to serve the customer and make it as easy as possible for them to obtain value from the company in exchange for revenues. Additionally, take care of the customer if they are unhappy, and give them a reason to come back and tell their friends about you.**

Some might be thinking, "I'm just a _____; how can I ask questions like these or worry about the bigger picture?" I'll talk about this more in later chapters. The idea is that you must stand for something and anchor your point of views in a professional setting in something that is a constant. Since the very beginning of trade and commerce all the way to the present day of selling software as a service, humans have been, and always will be, the common denominator.

CHAPTER 9

BE STRATEGIC

———

Our power is in our ability to decide.

— BUCKMINSTER FULLER

This chapter was one of my favorites to write. Out of all the terms I could try to use to describe myself, I landed on "strategic" a few years ago, and it stuck.

I get asked a lot about how people can be more strategic. Are there books to read? Are there classes they can take? Everyone wants to be more strategic, even those in actual strategic positions at companies.

As stated earlier, "In one survey of 10,000 senior leaders, 97 percent of them said that being strategic was the leadership behavior most important to their organization's success. And yet in another study, a full 96 percent of the leaders surveyed said they lacked the time for strategic thinking."[43]

---

43   Dorie Clark, "If Strategy Is So Important, Why Don't We Make Time for It?" *Harvard Business*

That statistic always makes me chuckle. It's a page from my life. I think it's important for leaders to be strategic. This is a state of mind in any situation you are in—at home, school, work, and everywhere else.

It's worth starting with a dictionary definition of strategy. According to Merriam-Webster, the first definition of strategy is the science and art of employing the political, economic, psychological, and military forces of a nation or group of nations to afford the maximum support to adopted policies in peace or war.

What in the world? How does this apply to the business world?

Imagine that a company is a sovereign nation (whether it's public or private, it doesn't matter). Strategy is the means by which a company maintains its status in a world of companies (also known as the industry or nation in which it exists). I'll spare you, dear reader, from my inner political science geek.

In my own words, strategy is solving problems while taking into account the big picture. This skill is so critical to being a leader in any capacity.

A big part of doing strategy in a professional setting is doing discovery. In some cases, that can be a very formal discovery with a process and charts and maps and spreadsheets. In other cases, it can be informal, simply trying to learn how a business operates, how teams collaborate, how customers

Review, June 21, 2018.

feel about something, and what the market/competitors are doing in that space.

FIRST, DO YOUR HOMEWORK

I work with clients who are developing their e-commerce experiences. Many times, they pigeonhole this effort into one of two departments: marketing or IT, or sometimes both. Why is this a problem? In order to create an effective e-commerce experience and compete with the likes of Amazon or other disruptive digital-first brands, it would behoove companies to integrate all relevant parts of an organization when planning, building, and delivering the experience.

As much as we'd like to believe that marketing and IT have a holistic view of the business, chances are they've tried but cannot always get all their stakeholders to agree with each other or with them. The battle of the budget is ever-present; who gets what part of the budget and who goes about making those decisions?

One big misconception about strategy is that you can go into a situation and simply start solving problems.

That could not be further from the truth.

When I get asked to be the strategist on a project for a client, I start by asking the client (and our internal team) a lot of questions, such as:

- Who needs to be involved?
  - *Then make some requests to speak to additional people to get a holistic view.*
- What about the customers? How will this impact their experience?
  - *At the end of the day, the customers need to be the winner.*
- Who are the competitors to consider?
  - *The clients may mention companies they'd want to look out for or learn from.*
  - *Keep your options and eyes open outside of this short-list. It's your job to look out for what can come from left field.*
- What type of research has already been done that should be considered?
  - *If the client has already invested some work on this project, we should leverage it and be stewards of the client's resources.*
- Is there any documentation on the current state of affairs/processes/etc.?
  - *It doesn't make sense if your eventual solution contra-dicts what exists. It should improve upon or comple-ment what currently exists.*
- What are some limitations you might have to keep in mind?
  - It would be better to know *major things earlier than to learn later. That's not to say that things won't come up later, but at least the client knows they can be trans-parent with you.*
- What, exactly, are we trying to accomplish?
  - *If no one can answer this, should you or your team start building something?*

- Who will be impacted by any decisions made through this process? Are they involved in this process?
  - *Many a project has come to a halt because the time and resource implication on other teams was not accounted for at the get-go.*
  - *While it's important to get buy-in from your client's higher-ups, it's equally important to get buy-in from your client's peers and counterparts in other departments. Politics in an organization is a real thing but not necessarily a bad thing.*
- What does success mean?
  - *This one is hard. Everyone must agree on the definition of success. You, your team, your client, their team, their peers, and their boss.*
  - *It must be measurable so you know when you achieve success.*

This list scratches the surface of the things I would want to uncover at the very beginning of client engagement. Of course, if your client is not expecting someone to be a formal strategist, these questions might seem unusual. Be sure to read the situation you are in before asking such directed questions. A strategist will be in a position to do so. Others may have to tread lightly in certain circumstances.

In addition to asking these questions, I would do research of my own online, having general conversations with people from my network if it's a consumer-facing product, and look at the industry and other industries that might have similar business models, value propositions, etc. I would attempt to look at every possible angle and just absorb and learn.

I HAVE ONE THOUSAND PAGES OF NOTES, NOW WHAT?

When I was in graduate school, one of my first classes was Consumer Insights, taught by a great professor named Michelle Weinberger. She taught us how to do ethnographic research and then code the themes to understand consumers.

Ethnographic studies are a research methodology borrowed from the field of sociology that results in a qualitative description of human behavior based on fieldwork.[44]

Another major part of being a strategist is the ability to organize what you're learning into themes. In data analysis terms, you are a human machine trying to put structure and order around unstructured data. Why not start putting the information into themes the moment you receive the information? That's one time-saving method you could use, but sometimes you miss out on a potentially different way to solve something if you rush to conclusions early on.

The idea is to start identifying themes and making connections with information gathered from different parts of your research/homework.

A lot of my job as a strategist is gathering this information, presenting it to my clients in an easily digestible format, then facilitating solution-creation within multifunctional groups. Eventually, the desired effect is that it helps people, particularly my clients, make decisions for their company.

---

44 Department of Sociology - Northwestern University, "Ethnography," Accessed April 25, 2020.

A MAP TO EVERYWHERE

Journey maps, mind maps, thematic maps, road maps, strategy maps, impact maps (shoutout to Shakeel Mohammed who introduced me to this one), just to name a few, all have something in common. They all organize the information learned about a situation or a company.

But why maps? The definition of strategy is the science and art of employing the political, economic, psychological, and military forces of a **nation or group of nations** to afford the maximum support to adopted policies in peace or war. Maps used to be the starting point, with other elements layered onto them to communicate tactics and plans with rulers, generals, diplomats, etc.

Being the history nerd that I am, my close friend Angela Abalos and I went to the Churchill War Museum in London during our last trip to the UK. Winston Churchill was the prime minister of the United Kingdom during World War II and the five years immediately after the war. I loved the entire museum (which was also Churchill's underground wartime bunker), where Churchill created a strategy to inform operations.

I can gush on about the museum for days, but here are some important things I wanted to highlight. Because technology was not what it is now, being strategic during wartime was done the old-fashioned way. In a way, how we create business strategy is still being done in a similar manner, with the exception that we make our maps on computers now. Nothing is wrong with this, but the strategist in me was secretly (and publicly) having a field day.

As I was geeking out, I arrived at some very simple observations about how Churchill had organized his wartime headquarters:

- People were responsible for gathering information.
- People were responsible for documenting what they learned.
- People were then problem-solving and providing Churchill with options.
- The brilliant leader that he was, Churchill moved swiftly with his **decision-making.**
- The decisions were then quickly documented on maps and letters and other formats and communicated to those who needed to know what to do next.

Businesses can learn a lot from this...informed decision-making in a life-or-death environment creates an unmatched sense of urgency.

Perhaps in another life, I will write a book about wartime finances, because companies don't always have the luxury of the wartime budgets many leaders are equipped with. That creates the perfect opportunity for creativity and innovation. But more on that some other time.

"WAIT, WHAT IF I'M NOT A STRATEGIST?"

If you take one thing out of all this, it's that all the strategy in the world is pointless if it does not help leaders make decisions for the collective good.

Many of you might say something like, "I'm not a strategist. My title is analyst or project manager or something else." You can be strategic in any role, in any part of your life. If you're not a formal strategist, it might be hard to get all the answers you are looking for, and that's alright for that brief period.

The goal when aiming to be a strategist is to practice thinking like one and fine-tune your problem-solving skills.

For example, if you are a content creator for a company, you may be given a content brief that tells you who your audience is, the purpose of the content, where it would be used, what the call to action would be, etc. If this is not presented to you, then those might be some good questions to start with. In addition, do your own research. Figure out what the customer would naturally see before and after seeing the content.

Experienced content creators probably have an intuition with which they approach content creation. It's a blend of art and science that comes with practice and having the right context.

I come across this quite a bit whenever I attend alumni events at my alma mater. I meet current students who want to get into data science and analytics roles but want to learn about strategy roles as their end goal. A few years ago, IBM predicted that data science roles will soar 28 percent by 2020.[45]

Data scientists and analysts have the information, and plenty of it. If they can tell stories with that information, a cohesive

45   Columbus, Louis, "IBM Predicts Demand for Data Scientists Will Soar 28% by 2020," *Forbes*, May 13, 2017.

story that helps people make decisions, that is key. It's not enough to use a data visualization tool to create charts and graphic analysis. A human being must piece those together with the larger business story for it to make sense. Too much data can create analysis paralysis on everyone's part and turn into noise. Not enough relevant data can lessen confidence in the insights. Finding a balance in the form of a well-structured story can make all the difference.

Many experts in the data world might advise that people must start with the questions they are trying to answer to avoid falling into the data analysis rabbit hole. For businesses, that must be grounded in something that would be considered the ultimate truth: the customer.

Whatever your job is, learn about the customer your company is ultimately serving. Everything you do should be about them, even if you're not directly asked to do that. Use that as context to do good work. This is leveraging your social skills, empathy, and motivation at a completely different level.

CHAPTER 10

DISRUPTION VS. EVOLUTION

———

Disruption is a very broad, unstructured concept. Every person and every company can define disruption differently. That is why I find it to be an important topic to address being disruptive unintentionally can become a liability instead of an asset. If all you become known for is disrupting, then that is fine, but it can become uncomfortable and quite lonely if you feel like others cannot understand where you are coming from all the time.

For the past half a decade or longer, all businesses, especially large, complex, lethargic, bureaucratic companies, have been encouraged to disrupt or be disrupted. There is a constant fear of being Amazoned out of existence (yes, I just used Amazon as a verb because, why not?).

However, not many people talk about how uncomfortable it is to be disruptive. I remember when I went from working at Accenture's Customer Innovation Center (where the conversations were about disrupting and how to enable disruption) to Merkle, I noticed a shift in client's comfort levels at disrupting. They were not hiring a performance management company to help them disrupt anything. They wanted help measuring and optimizing what they already had in their fully operational business.

In the process, if we happened to identify opportunities to innovate and disrupt, great. If not, it was important to maintain forward motion in a project, team, or company.

FOR CURRENT LEADERS/MANAGERS

Companies traditionally considered disruptive could be large or small, but they are most certainly nimble. They tend to hire people who can be comfortable with fluidity and change as things mature in their business. Those who are not comfortable with this type of fluidity typically end up at companies that already have a solid business model and a traditional organizational structure with defined processes.

However, if large companies who want to disrupt the marketplace continue to hire the same types of people, they will be unable to disrupt the market because, well, they are filled with people who don't like change! It's uncomfortable for those used to the status quo, and those who've benefited from the status quo.

Many individuals at large organizations can be, and should be, agents of change. Change agents are those individuals who ruffle the feathers in their curmudgeonly companies and can be conduits for disruption. This is where things get complicated. Some companies reward this type of behavior and look for individuals to have these types of change-agent-like characteristics. Other companies claim they are looking for people with different points of view, but their performance measures do not reward people who try to do things differently. They do not have the right internal structure.

Companies will need to start rewarding people for taking risks while also hiring people who have the desire not necessarily to disrupt but to solve problems objectively. If that happens to disrupt, then so be it. If it doesn't, then that's alright.

So the real challenge is not always disrupting the marketplace but disrupting the old way of doing things internally within an organization. If you encourage the latter in your team or company, it will help you identify opportunities to solve problems differently.

But what do you look for when looking for change agents? People like this are probably right under your nose, but you don't look at them that way. Take a moment to reflect on who on your team already fits this bill before looking elsewhere:

- Do you know a strategic, innovative thinker?
- Are they obsessed with the customer?
- Can they think at an ecosystem-level?
- Can they come up with ways to leverage existing partnerships?
- Are they curious about things that might challenge the status quo?
- Can they easily collaborate with others who are not from your team, department, or even company?

- Do they have a growth mindset? That is, are they willing to listen, learn, and explore?

FOR THOSE TRYING TO BE CHANGE AGENTS

Does the list above sound like you? Are you all these things but people just don't know it yet? If these things don't describe you, how do you become a change agent?

First, stop trying to be what others want you to be. This can be people in your family, your friends, or even a mentor. You are not your job title or your position in the family structure. Start to define who you are yourself. This is especially true for women and minorities.

For example, I have had many mentors in my career. One of those mentors kept envisioning me working with her but didn't know what role I would play other than a glorified assistant. Had this been the actual position I applied for, that would be have been fine. It worked when I was first trying to get into the digital consulting industry, but over time, it didn't seem like the right role for me. Regardless of the title, I was always supporting her vision. I wasn't allowed to envision on my own.

Many years later, if I reached out to this person for a job, she would probably still see me as that bright-eyed, bushy-tailed recent graduate looking for validation. She is a close friend but will probably never see me as the person I am now. And that's OK. I do not define myself based on her validation of me anymore.

You will have to do some reflecting and choose to accept or reject things that you've believed about yourself and your role in the world/marketplace.

Secondly, don't lead the way others want you to lead. Develop your own style. Easier said than done when we have already established that everything we've learned about leadership has come from those around us.

While this is true, if someone you respect does something or uses a management style you do not agree with, you do not have to embrace it. More importantly, you do not have to take that element on as a part of your own leadership style because you think it was effective. It might have been effective for that person, but it might not work the same way for you, especially if you did not agree with it in the first place.

I have fallen victim to this myself. And I share this story with people all the time because it's a great example of two people being completely different, with different styles, achieving the same outcomes.

During my first job out of college, I had this wonderful manager. Her style was matter of fact with everyone around her, and she was so honest, sometimes it hurt. But I loved and respected her for that, and I still turn to her to be honest with me. Well, a big part of that first job required us to write emails with specific requests to external partners, who were mostly trade credit insurance underwriters. Because I was young and new, I was in training for almost a year. It was standard for new employees.

Writing these emails seemed informal, but we were making written requests and following them up with a phone call. I did not mind writing the email, but the phone call part used to scare me. I *hated* getting on the phone with these underwriters, most of whom I would love to talk to about personal things, but I hated talking business with them.

My manager helped me tighten up my emails a bit by taking out some of the flowery language I was so used to writing when I was trying to reach my minimum word counts for my essays in college. The flowery language had no place in business writing, and I learned that early on. I decided to keep that as a part of my style in the future.

Now came the phone part. My manager was such a powerful woman with a definitive presence on the phone and in person. I, on the other hand, could barely be heard on the phone sometimes. People on the other end would ask me to speak louder all the time. My manager called the underwriters, with whom she had been working with for so long, and quickly got to the point. Like, "Hey John, I need this limit approved by tonight. Ok, thanks, ciao."

Do you want to know what happened when I tried to do that? One of the underwriters called the founder of our company to tell him that I was rude, short, and inexperienced and that I needed to be taught how to work with the underwriters.

Little twenty-one-year-old me was mortified. Not only did I not like talking about business on the phone, but I was also emulating someone else's style and it didn't work. That's the first time I vowed not to be anyone other than myself.

I still had to have these phone conversations, but I started focusing on building relationships with people. Many of the underwriters were older than me by decades, and some of them were women. I decided that if I couldn't intimidate them into getting what I wanted, I would be kind through the process and still get what I want.

When I didn't get the decisions I wanted from them, I would ask them why. What could I have done differently? I tried to learn from them. So many times in the process of teaching me, they changed their mind. They started showing me how to tell a story from two pages of a financial statement. Over time, I could get on the phone with one of these underwriters and have the quick, "Hey Sarah, just sent you something. I need a decision on it by tomorrow afternoon. Thanks, bye," and it was fine because we knew each other by then. We had spent hours talking to each other, learning about each other's lives, and had lunch together when I visited New York. I built relationships with people, and that's how I started developing my leadership style.

This was in stark contrast to my manager, who is highly successful even to this day. People love her for the way she is and respect her working/leadership style.

You have to develop your own as well.

Leverage new credentials (not titles/degrees). I feel like I can say this because I have dropped a pretty penny on higher education not once, but twice. Those pieces of paper gave me confidence, but everything I learned after my formal schooling is the practical stuff that I still use to this day.

I learned early in my career the painful lesson that nobody has to give you the time of day because you went to this school or that school or have this degree or that degree. Don't tell my parents this, but most of the time, I'm not telling people about my degrees. I'm showing them my skills through my work.

A commonly held misconception is that getting a higher degree will suddenly transform you into a leader. Some programs focus on leadership development, and many of them have done wonders for helping people develop their leadership styles. But a certificate or degree won't guarantee that you'll be a leader.

Credibility, the honor system, and a growth mindset are your credentials in the new world. With more and more people working from home, people being given more autonomy, and companies needing people with new ideas, these three things will be your greatest advantages when coming across others with more stellar resumes than you.

Lastly, problem solve outside the line of duty. Read the situation but sometimes you don't have to wait for permission.

Many years ago, Walgreens was transitioning as an organization from Lotus Notes to Microsoft 365 and Outlook. My job was to address the tickets generated when internal users emailed or called when they were scheduled for the transition.

However, throughout my conversations with these individuals, I noticed that many of them didn't understand when I asked them to click this button or that button. The devices we were making the transitions on ranged from PCs to Macs to Blackberrys and iPhones. Some users were transitioning from device to device while also getting newly set up on their Microsoft Outlook account.

Considering that many people required visual aids, I created a guide with screenshots and step-by-step instructions on how to set up Microsoft Outlook on each device users might have. I shared these guides with my boss and the others on my team. Before addressing users' tickets, my team and I would send this guide so users had something to reference during our call.

Our department was measured by how many tickets we closed and how long it took for a ticket to be resolved. The guides helped us quickly troubleshoot the simpler cases, leaving us time to walk step by step through the more difficult tickets. The time it took users to set up their email accounts reduced significantly (instead of taking an hour and potential follow-up calls if the users could not continue, it only took about thirty minutes and one phone call).

The average number of open tickets at any given time went down as well since we resolved most of them quickly. Because of my attempts at making my own work more efficient, the others on my team benefited as well.

THE TAKEAWAY: DISRUPTION MAY NOT ALWAYS BE THE ANSWER, BUT WHEN IT IS, BE FEARLESS AND BE BOLD.

Don't wait for approval or validation. Take ownership. It's been said that it's better to apologize after the fact than to ask for permission. I think it's actually *hard* to move forward and make a decision without permission. However, when working through normal hierarchies, asking for permission many times implies *waiting*. Many a good person has died in the waiting room; the same is true of good ideas.

Good leaders *empower* their team members to make decisions on their own whenever possible. If you're waiting on a leader to make a decision for you, you're either going to wait forever, act without permission, or start putting together a case for why the leader should make this particular decision. This is where if you are strategic (explained in another chapter), you are less likely to need to apologize if you do decide to proceed without permission.

PART THREE

APPLYING THE ENTREPRENEURIAL LEADERSHIP PRINCIPLES

CHAPTER 11

ANCHORING YOURSELF

———

Some basic ground rules must be established for this part of the book. Some of these things might be obvious, but it's important to make note of them because they can get in the way of looking at situations differently. Some of these can come in the form of roadblocks, people who are difficult to work with, being unable to distinguish your managerial skills and leadership skills, and ensuring a safe work environment for everyone around you, especially those who might not readily stand up for themselves.

No linear format exists to incorporate all the principles of leadership that I shared previously. I have grouped them in a few different categories to demonstrate which ones come together in different environments. This chapter starts with anchoring yourself for success. Then, I walk through examples of applications in the workplace, in volunteer environments, and lastly how the principles play a part in measuring success.

USING YOUR MINDSET TO OVERCOME THE ROADBLOCKS

People I've spoken to share a generally accepted sentiment that you can have roadblocks to being a good leader. I would like to call these excuses.

Getting past these roadblocks or excuses is a big part of the growth needed to be a good leader. Excuses add up and making them regularly enough can lead to a negative work environment. People reacting to this negativity can take their frustrations out on each other. And all this can contribute to a toxic work environment. Once you get to toxicity, it's hard to reverse it.

Here are some examples of excuses people give for why they cannot be good leaders:

- Don't have the right staff
- Don't have enough information
- Don't have the budget
- Don't have vision or don't understand how vision applies to your team and your work
- Have a bad leader
- Have a crisis situation/PR issue
- Have a bad apple (or a few bad apples) who don't play well with others on the team; I have to work with jerks every day

What are some types of responses using the different appeals?

- Emotional – Slow down as a group, assess humans and their behavior. What is the roadblock?

- Logical – Logical appeals, if communicated effectively, can get your team on the same page to start moving quickly on given tasks or objectives. Once that is underway, a good leader can assess as needed and provide emotional support in a one-off fashion.
- Cooperative – this is where humans need group emotion and group logic to get things done. They may need immediate validation for their own ideas or may need the inspiration to come up with logical, tactical solutions.

How does this help with the jerks in the room, either a leader or a team member? Emotional and logical appeals may not always work one on one because the leader is pretty much convinced that they can never be wrong. Cooperative appeals can give you power in the form of numbers, but it requires some one-on-one diplomatic legwork.

BECOMING THE PEOPLE-PERSON WHEN YOU ARE THE JERK

Have you ever come across a situation where you think to yourself, "Wow, what a jerk!"

Even if you're not one to throw angry words around, it's hard to not run into these types of people at work or at other places.

But what if you *are* this person? What if you're the office jerk?

While learning about leadership from leaders is important, learning about leadership from those being led is more relevant when trying to determine what makes a good leader or a bad one.

As I reviewed recent survey responses to questions about why someone might not be a good leader, many of the negative qualities mentioned were a leader's personality traits, not actual management skills. They may or may not be professionally qualified to lead, but that's not what seemed to bother people. It's that they did not effectively communicate or manage their own emotions when leading and came off as being unkind.

Most jerks don't acknowledge that they are one; most of the time, they're not even aware that they are being jerks or they ignore the feedback. I also recently learned from a Red Table Talk episode that if someone develops a large number of narcissistic traits as a child or teen, it can never be reversed. Spooky!

That's terrifying. And with social media relying on people's need to be seen and seen only in a positive light, who knows what the next generation will look like?

If you are the office jerk, do you know why are you the office jerk? Are you alright with your aggressive (which is different from assertive) behavior coming off as confidence to the higher-ups so you can continue growing in your career on the backs of others?

Are you mature enough to acknowledge that you are, in fact, not a nice person? If you are willing to acknowledge your behavior and are interested in changing, then there is hope for you yet.

The simple act of reflecting on your own behavior implies that you are not trying to be a jerk, but you have not figured out a productive way to communicate with your team when in stressful situations. While I am not justifying being an asshole, self-awareness is a big step to personal and professional development.

Believe me, we have all been there.

REPRESENTING THE VOICELESS AND UNDERREPRESENTED

I've been lucky enough, even at my first company after college, IRC, to have wonderful people surround me in the workplace. In fact, at IRC, some people were one of the main reasons I stuck around as long as I did. It's important for me to remember and acknowledge some of the extraordinary people I met in my career.

The founders of IRC are both amazing human beings who worked every day to be excellent and reminded all us that we were working not just for us but for our children (at least the ones who had them). Some of my mentors early in my career at that company were some of the strongest, most resilient women I had ever met. They were the first ones to notice that I was painfully shy and that I needed some help (OK, a lot of help) coming out of my shell.

Earlier, I recounted my time at Accenture's Customer Innovation Center. Many people work at large companies, many of them in my personal network, who feel like a robot, repeating the same mundane activity every day and feeling no sense of purpose. I did not feel that way when at Accenture. In fact, I could not have thought of a better way to repeat a series of extremely fun tasks across a variety of different subject areas to continue to gain confidence in myself.

When thinking about people, I had many good ones to pick from....heck, when even thinking about why I felt like I was good enough to write this book or ever feel like a leader, I think specifically about my current manager, Christina Lagoda.

We hit it off right away. She inherited me as a direct report, which could have gone many different ways. I am an analytical, not visually creative but still creative in other ways, human-centered design strategist just trying to find her way in the world of brilliant technologists at an e-commerce consulting firm.

She comes off as being quiet herself at first meeting. However, when she speaks, she can effortlessly toggle between logical, emotional, and cooperative appeals in a positive manner. She also looked to hire people, regardless of their specific hard skill sets, who could also toggle between the three or at least aspire to do so at some point.

She attracted several wonderful people to work with her because they knew her from previous roles. As a result, our team is stronger than it has ever been before...and has grown significantly from when we both first joined the company. She puts her people first and looks at them as equals, even when it comes down to getting work done. She is the first one to roll up her sleeves alongside those who report to her. Just like many of the managers I've had before, Christina too has played a major role in seeing the potential in me that even I couldn't see and helping me evolve my Leadership UVP.

How does this relate to the voiceless and underrepresented? If I did not have an advocate for my career, like Christina at SMITH, among others, I don't think I would have naturally seen what I was capable of. It's not that my parents weren't encouraging (despite my griping about them) or my friends. It's just that no one could find the right way to harness my skills until certain leaders did so for me.

The home equation is particularly poignant for younger individuals, women, and minorities. When I was going through some transitions in life a few years ago, people like Christina and SMITH's human resources director worked with me to help me shift to a part-time employee temporarily until things settled down a bit. And I felt comfortable enough going to them at the time. A good leader recognizes that one cannot avoid what happens at home, and sometimes it does impact our productivity.

Privilege is a *major* discussion point and the reason so many of us feel it's so hard to kill it in the marketplace and feel like we have a voice or feel represented. Privilege can come in many forms. Our baggage can set us up to fail if we do not address it appropriately. This is why getting your *self* sorted out early on is beneficial to you, personally and professionally.

WHEN TO BE STRATEGIC AND WHEN TO BE TACTICAL

Within any role, you must be able to do both, depending on the situation. How easily can you toggle between the two? Do they sometimes blend into each other? Most definitely.

If you want to learn more about management and leadership, I would recommend reading several great books written by John P. Kotter, a renowned author, leader, and professor at Harvard University. One of those books, *A Force for Change: How Leadership Differs From Management*, Kotter explains exactly that.[46] While the book was written in 1990, the concepts are still something that resonate as wisdom within the business community.

Traditional organizations saw management and leadership as two distinct areas of a company, potentially even filled by two different individuals or groups of people. Today, regardless of the size of the company, the same person managing concrete outcomes like task and project completion is also indirectly responsible for making sure people are motivated and inspired. Sometimes they may be responsible for creating the vision, and other times they're responsible for communicating the vision to their teams. The same individual may have to toggle between their managerial responsibilities (that lean more toward the tactical) and their leadership responsibilities (that lean more toward the strategic). The same person would use both skillsets, depending on the situation and the desired outcome. And

---

46 John P. Kotter. *A Force For Change: How Leadership Differs From Management.* New York: Free Press, 1990.

ultimately they intersect when both are being utilized at their best.[47]

As a **manager**, one would be responsible for maintaining order and consistency within a team, project or organization. One would need to plan and budget to anticipate financial and resource requirements needed to complete a certain set or tasks or to complete a project, for example. A manager would organize people around completing tasks and would utilize their staff accordingly. Their primary role is to control variables in each environment and solve problems where needed, all the while ensuring that the group completes the tasks in the timeline required.[48]

As a **leader**, one would be responsible for creating change and motion, usually a forward motion. One would establish direction and vision for their organization or team and set strategies and expectations. A leader's role is to align people around common goals, obtain commitments towards achieving those goals, build teams and collaborative environments. The leader's primary role is to motivate and inspire, empower people who report to them and provide the intangible needs that ultimately drive people to follow the leader's directives.[49]

How would that work in a real-life scenario in an organization?

When my husband and I both worked at Nushii, the sushi burrito start-up in Los Angeles, California, we both played

---

47   John Kotter, "What Leaders Really Do," in *HBR's 10 Must Reads On Leadership* (Boston: Harvard Business School Publishing, 2011), 26-33.

48   ibid.

49   ibid.

different roles. My role was more of a customer experience expert and my husband's role was operational. My world was digital and sometimes theoretical and my husband's was more in-person and tactical. However, we had decided as a leadership team that every employee should not only know what their tasks are, but why they are doing it the way that they are doing it.

When my husband, Alykhan Samji, started each shift in the beginning, he would remind everyone that we are here to serve the customer. Every sushi burrito we wrap, every word we say, every time we smile or wipe down a table, it is for our customer. This is also then how our social media manager handled social chat conversations when customers asked a question or wrote a bad review. Every day, for every employee, was about completing tasks while keeping the bigger picture in mind. And while a leader's job is to create change and motion where needed, our anchor never changed: the customer.

This eventually expanded into the dozens of off-site events that our company hosted, our catering and delivery orders. It eventually became a part of how our newest employee ended up being trained by our other employees. Change came with the addition of new delivery, pick-up and catering partnerships. It changed how tasks were managed. But because everyone knew that we were trying to serve the customer, and at that moment the customer wanted to order our product through their delivery service app, our staff jumped right on it.

At an organizational leadership level, I was responsible for strategy and marketing and my husband was responsible for communicating and implementing the cultural expectations to the staff. However, neither of us could do our jobs without understanding each other's world. I worked many shifts on the line to learn about how long it took to make a sushi burrito, I washed dishes and mopped the floors to know what it felt like to work there, I tasted everything new that came out of research and development, I drank every new beverage that we tried to sell to know what my brand stood for from the inside out. Meanwhile, my husband talked to customers, read online reviews to learn how to improve the product and processes, jumped on the latest trends of online ordering and built partnerships, despite a lot of those responsibilities being a strategist's responsibility.

There were times when the strategist in me needed to be able to manage tasks when we were on an off-site. There were other times when my husband had to motivate and inspire the team when they were exhausted and we had back-to-back caterings. We had to toggle between managing and leading constantly.

The main idea here is that many people believe that once they have mastered the art of managing people and tasks that they are bona fide leaders. They may have the foundation to be leaders but there are many other responsibilities that a leader has than managing people and tasks, as noted earlier.

In the context of this book, different appeals are needed for each type of role too. When managing tasks or people completing tasks, such as in a project, managers tend to lean on their logical or emotional appeals to influence individuals. This generally works until various tasks or workstreams have dependencies with each other. In that case, managers must rely on their cooperative appeal. They must inspire and empower the people they are managing to work with each other, as opposed to working by themselves.

CHAPTER 12

THE WORKPLACE

—

The workplace can be defined as many different things for different people. Some people work from their homes, cars, or cafes, while others work in offices, manufacturing facilities, banks, classrooms, or hospitals. The nature of work, where it is done, and the number of hours one spends working, mentally at least, has changed a lot in the past decade or so. Even when someone works from an office, they may often take their work home with them, checking emails on their phones or responding to calls from the bosses or colleagues after hours.

What does working hard even mean nowadays? Is it measured in the number of hours one spends working? Or is it measured in how many tasks are completed? Busyness is sometimes used interchangeably with accomplishment. If someone is constantly busy, they must be important.

I used to feel that way too before I finished college. I used to be impressed when people had a work cell phone and a personal cell phone until I had both at one point in my career. It's not a glamorous thing at all. You basically had to be accessible to your bosses and your clients all the time. There was no break or boundary between work life and personal life. So then what does all the busyness and grunt work result in?

In the race to complete tasks, perform well on reviews, and meet deadlines, we forget to see the big picture. In this chapter, I talk through some ways to maintain focus on the required tasks while also keeping the longer-term vision in your line of sight.

While many of my examples are from a traditional office setting or a potential remote work setting, the high-level concepts should help in many different professions or workplace environments. This section is particularly focused on roles where one receives monetary compensation for the work they do (as opposed to voluntary service, which will be covered elsewhere).

Everything discussed in this chapter can apply to both emerging and experienced leaders. Emerging leadership has nothing to do with age. Based on the past ten years, people are changing their careers frequently. That being said, someone in their forties and fifties could be an emerging leader because they just joined a new line of work or are trying to increase a certain skill set even if they've had years of experience doing something else. Experienced leaders could be as young as a twenty-year-old who started her company from her parent's garage at twelve years old. We've all heard those stories about young entrepreneurs leading hundreds of people before they turn thirty.

I may use examples of people in emerging leadership situations, but it can be useful for all types of leaders in the workplace.

REMAIN FOCUSED: EXPECTATIONS FOR PROGRESS

One of the biggest complaints I hear from experienced leaders about emerging leaders is about expectations. Experienced leaders wonder if they are communicating expectations properly. Emerging leaders might expect more in terms of affirmation and compensation, and even leadership opportunities. Experienced leaders might feel that emerging leaders are not fulfilling the responsibilities of their roles but still expect more rewards than they might deserve.

What is an example of this?

LinkedIn has a great feature that tells you exactly how qualified you are for a specific role. No one can be a 100-percent match for a job, so around 70–80 percent is a pretty good place to be, in my opinion. On paper, the odds can look pretty good. For example, when looking at a role in Healthcare Marketing, I ranked in the Top 10 percent of many applicants. Of the skills I had listed on LinkedIn, mine matched only three of the ones that the recruiter wanted for this particular role. I could probably check off on the rest as well, with lower proficiency on my part in "Healthcare Marketing" and "Contract Negotiation," but if I had to, I could learn those skills.

So the hiring manager and the human resources specialist may have decided to list these things to best describe the position they're trying to fill. Once hired, if I'm asked to create a deliverable or conduct an activity, I need to be able to do the things I claim I know how to do.

That seems obvious, doesn't it? But how one defines analytical skills and customer experience skills can vary from person to person and company to company. The interview process should hopefully help all parties understand what is expected, but many times it's not always clear.

Basically, you are being hired to complete very specific tasks. Let's say you need to complete ten tasks. The expectations should be based on the problems you are being hired to solve.

Your manager has hired you to solve for these	You are currently solving these	Your manager is expecting to compensate / reward /affirm your work for these	You are expecting compensation / reward / affirmation for these
Task 1 to be completed proficiently	X	X	X
Task 2 to be completed proficiently	X	X	X
Task 3 to be completed proficiently	X	X	X
Task 4 to be completed proficiently		X	X
Task 5 to be completed proficiently		X	X
Task 6 to be completed proficiently	X	X	X

Your manager has hired you to solve for these	You are currently solving these	Your manager is expecting to compensate / reward /affirm your work for these	You are expecting compensation / reward / affirmation for these
Task 7 to be completed proficiently		X	X
Task 8 – Nice to have	X	X	X
Task 9 – Nice to have	X	X	X
Task 10 – Nice to have		X	X
	New task you have created for yourself that doesn't contribute to solving the original tasks you were hired for		X
	Another new task you have created for yourself that doesn't contribute to solving the original tasks you were hired for		X
	Other projects that you think will contribute to your company's objectives without getting clearance from your manager		X

I saw this happen at the sushi burrito start-up quite a bit. We had younger employees, some fresh out of high school, and others still in college who expected to be promoted or get a raise when they were not doing the jobs they were originally hired to do. Some of the jobs they were responsible for involved prep work, front-of-the-house work like making sushi burritos, cleaning up the countertops, greeting customers, sweeping the floor at the end of a shift and between shifts, and taking out the trash, just to name a few. Why did they want a raise or a bonus? Because they posted about the product on social media. Yes, it was a fun, glamorous job and was growing the brand, but we already had an intern from UCLA doing that job for us. If they did the tasks they were hired to do exceptionally well, and went above and beyond, then they could be considered for raises, bonuses, or promotions.

The best way for emerging leaders to set themselves up for success is clearly stating what they hope to achieve every week or month or quarter and ensure that it matches what your manager is expecting of you. At that time, you should make the case for why some additional tasks will be good for the company or will enhance your work experience. Your manager should have full transparency into what else you're spending your time on, and as long as you can complete the work that is your responsibility, you can move on to other tasks you have set for yourself.

Set expectations properly, meet them, and then exceed them. If you have joined a mostly great company that has some flaws, give it a chance. If you are not happy with the culture, then play a part in creating a culture around you. If the only thing you end up doing aside from your daily tasks is to enhance a company's culture, then you have set that company up with a new standard for excellence and a foundation to continue building upon.

EVOLVING BEYOND THE JOB DESCRIPTION

Once you've established yourself as an expert at the tasks you've been assigned, you can find efficiencies in completing your tasks and focus on learning new things or developing your leadership skills. Many companies encourage employees to do this and may even provide a structured format to do so. I would highly encourage emerging leaders to take advantage of this, once they've gotten a good handle on their primary responsibilities, of course.

This is a great opportunity to ask your manager if you could learn from or assist with any different projects. Other companies have knowledge resources where you can learn about the company, its history, other types of work being done, and so on. Some companies may even have employees blog about certain topics to help them grow their personal brand.

Start with things you didn't know how to do when you first joined. For example, if you have never worked on putting together a project plan from beginning to end, ask your manager to teach you how to do that when you are not in a crunch for time. See if they can share resources with you to learn more or introduce you to someone in the company who could teach you a new skill.

Knowledge Is Power but Only if You Share It

Knowledge sharing or knowledge repositories are becoming a common practice within large organizations. It helps with creating an institutional memory, especially in an environment where job-hopping is so common. But what does that have to do with *your* leadership abilities?

I have encountered this in more than one way in the workplace, where individuals will only share the information they think is necessary for someone to do their job well. I think so much is wrong with this. I have worked in many types of companies. In some companies, the leadership shared *every last detail* about the company, including how much money everyone made. That turned out to be a bad idea over time. Other companies provided access to a lot of information, but it was unstructured, so it was extremely difficult to find what you needed. And then you had those companies where you only get the version of the truth that someone thought you needed to do a good job.

Here is where this could go wrong, for example, in a consulting environment. Suppose three people are on a team—Ms. Kelly Know-It-All, Mr. Justin O.K. Fine, and Ms. Anjali Where-Do-I-Start?

Kelly has the relationship with the client. She learns everything she needs to learn from the client, documents very little from the conversations, and shares even less with her teammates.

Justin, who is a technologist, might be used to this and may just want to keep things moving. He is so busy, he just wants to complete his deliverables, with maybe a couple of follow-up questions, and move on.

Anjali, who is a strategist/business consultant/who cares what her title is, has been hired to do some macro-level problem solving for the client. However, Kelly seems to have already decided which problems need solving and tells Anjali that she should focus on just one or two things.

The product or items delivered to the client are then extremely short-sighted and incomplete. Additionally, there is no institutional knowledge for new team members who join on either side (the client side or the consultant side). This sets the stage for a very weak relationship with the client, where it starts to become apparent that communication and transparency are not your company's strong suit.

It's just not a good way to lead. The title of this book is *In Power to Empower*. Sharing knowledge is a big part of empowering through the power of knowledge. I told my teammates in the past that I'd make them all strategists and give them the tools I use on projects. Other strategists I have worked with would rather keep that information to themselves. That might give them perceived power for a short amount of time, but in the long run, it does not help establish trust in the team you are part of.

WHAT DOES A LEADER DO? WHAT IS THEIR FOCUS?

I decided to have a chat with Dr. Asif Ashiqali, who has a PhD in Organizational and Leadership Development from The Chicago School of Professional Psychology. His family and mine have known each other for more than a couple of decades, and his sister, Asma, and I went to high school together.

We never really talked about work when we all hung out as friends because he was my friend's older brother. I learned about his illustrious career through the course of my interview with him. He started his career in manufacturing, where he was a supervisor for a few years. Then he went to IBM and was a technology consultant. Since then, he has been in operations and leadership at the University of Illinois and has done teaching and consulting work in this space.

According to Dr. Ashiqali, a leader is someone who gives direction but is also involved with, or at least knowledgeable of, operations on a day-to-day basis. Such leaders:

- Facilitate the overall process
- Enable transparency
- Maintain a thirty-thousand-foot view all the way down to the grassroots level
- Have knowledge of everything or should find a way to learn

Additionally, someone in mid-level management or the C-suite level doesn't sit on top and command people to do things...they get their hands dirty where needed to get the job done but have enough visibility to continue to direct large groups of people.

All the experience you obtain prior to becoming a formal leader helps you lead better rather than assuming that all the petty grunt work was a thing of the past. It makes you a well-rounded and grounded leader.

People who have started their own companies can probably attest to this. I've heard many younger folks say, "I want to be my own boss and start my own company." If that's how they escape the grunt work, then that's the wrong way to do it. There is no shortcut to becoming an experienced leader aside from going through those experiences.

WHAT DOES USING YOUR NEW [SUPER] POWER LOOK LIKE?

If knowledge is power and sharing it is empowering, then what does using your new [super] power of soft skills look like?

Once you've obtained a reputation for being a good employee who does your job well, and for being an avid learner and thinker, people will start asking your opinion. They'll want to include you and your perspective in the exciting new projects happening within the company.

When this starts happening, keep some important things in mind that recaps many things mentioned earlier:

- Be sure to keep fulfilling your stated responsibilities.
- Look at situations holistically; mindfulness is not simply a mental health ritual; it's the means through which you acknowledge *all things* around you.
- Get ahead of things, especially when you have to deliver uncomfortable news to a manager, customer, or client. Do not try to avoid the topic, lest it become a bigger problem and you get reprimanded for not bring it up earlier.

- You might make mistakes along the way, and that is completely fine. Open yourself up to feedback and learn. This should be your attitude for the rest of your career.
- When you start transitioning into being a leader will be unclear. It will probably happen gradually and informally, as you lead people on an ad hoc assignment or project.
- Pick and choose your battles. This is not only about putting up a good fight if you have a chance of winning it. It's also about using up your resources or social or political capital for a cause where the odds of winning are slim; why not focus on issues that help you win in the long-term?
- Be transparent. Communicate the "why" for all decisions with those you are leading to establish trust in your teams.

Maybe it will take you a few different jobs or companies to get to this point. Sometimes you are in a role to pay your bills until you find your dream job. That's alright. Nobody's dream job starts off as CEO unless you start your own company. Even then, there are many opportunities to fail and chances to learn.

Don't use anyone's measure of what success means or what age you should reach success. Finding a workplace that enables you to be the best version of yourself is probably the most important thing to do. If that means you move to another company or start your own, then so be it.

CHAPTER 13

VOLUNTEER ENVIRONMENTS

———

I wanted to include a chapter focused on volunteer environments as an homage to those that often gave me the confidence boost I lacked in my day job.

I have served in my religious community in a formal volunteer capacity for at least the past fifteen years, focusing both on local projects and initiatives as well as national ones over time. I have had moments of joy through my volunteer work, as well as moments of frustration. Most recently, I have been serving in the National Leadership Team for the Ismaili Professionals Network (IPN).

IPN was created over a decade ago to connect Ismaili professionals. Here is a quick summary of who the Ismailis are: "The Shia Imami Ismaili Muslims, generally known as the Ismailis, belong to the Shia branch of Islam. The Shia form one of the two major interpretations of Islam, the Sunni being the other. The Ismailis live in over 25 different countries, mainly in Central and South Asia, Africa, the Middle East, Europe, North America and Australia, and number approximately 20 million. The Ismailis are thus a transnational community who are responsible citizens of the countries where they live."[50]

Overall, I've gained more than I've lost with these experiences, so I hope all types of leaders will explore it as a way to give back and continue learning in a low-risk environment (getting fired from a volunteer role can have very different repercussions in your life than getting fired from your paid job).

Community and nonprofit volunteer opportunities are a great place to learn new hard skills, do something good for the community, and even exercise softer skills like those noted earlier in this book. This is also a place where people may lead largely with emotion because usually an individual, an ideology, or both has drawn people to the volunteer efforts.

Some communities or nonprofits tend to rely on a rigid hierarchy to create some form of order in an otherwise loosely structured environment. When people cannot get fired, fear of a tarnished reputation, shame for being deemed incompetent, or isolation (feeling like not belonging anymore) can be factors used to lead and be led.

Here are some ways to succeed in a volunteer environment, especially as a lot of volunteer work is done remotely.

---

50   The.Ismaili, "The Ismaili Community," accessed April 25, 2020.

SET EXPECTATIONS AS A VOLUNTEER

Setting expectations, just as in paid workplace environments, is incredibly important for people volunteering as well as those relying on volunteers to satisfy the needs of a community or nonprofit organization. As this book is for emerging as leaders, chances are you are trying to gather as many skills as you possibly can. However, it's also important to establish some expectations as a volunteer.

Prior to starting, put everything you intend to help an organization with in writing. The number of hours required, what you are specifically responsible for, if there are other expectations like in-person events, financial contributions required, and whether you'll need to use your personal network as part of the role are all things to learn about right away.

For example, one of the nonprofits I was involved with expected all volunteers to also help with fundraising. Some people on the team who were helping with the website or writing content were helping because they were friends with the founder, but they weren't necessarily comfortable using their personal networks to fundraise. That is an important expectation to set early on.

RESPECT THE TIME AND KNOWLEDGE OF VOLUNTEERS AS A LEADER

It's very easy to forget when someone is in a volunteer environment that individuals are not getting paid for their time and knowledge. They are offering it out of the goodness of their heart and potentially other reasons related to their personal or professional growth.

Sometimes volunteers may sign up to serve ten hours a week but then get roped into doing more than they signed up for and end up working twenty or thirty hours per week. This might work once or twice, but, eventually, that volunteer won't be able to sustain volunteering while also maintaining other parts of their life. And most of the time, they will have to choose their day jobs or their families if they don't choose their volunteer work. If they choose their volunteer work, they will resent it because it will be a source of unhappiness due to their sense of obligation.

As a leader, if you have set expectations with a volunteer that they will be contributing ten hours of their time per week, for example, err on the side of using up 9.5 hours, so it can be a more sustainable part of their life. This is especially true of professionals who also have side hustles who also wish to volunteer their time. Get more volunteers to get the job done and respect them for what they can contribute.

The same goes for resources or expertise. I have paid my dues as a professional, ran many meetings large and small, and can make a pretty mean PowerPoint presentation on the surface. What I am truly capable of is looking at the bigger picture as opposed to some of the tactical things I might volunteer my time for...Don't assume I am not capable of more because I'm volunteering my time for a lesser skilled task. Maybe that's just not how I want to volunteer my time.

INCENTIVIZE VOLUNTEERS AS A LEADER

Leading volunteers is a whole new realm that has not been fully explored by leadership books. Intrinsic things bind the team together. If these things are not communicated properly, a team of volunteers may feel less engaged. This has become an even bigger challenge as nonprofits and religious communities try to attract younger people, many times young professionals, to either be a part of their teams or manage major portions of their efforts.

Volunteers can be motivated by many things not related to monetary rewards that can be equally as effective.

- **A sense of belonging.** One way to supplement in-person volunteer work where they can get their sense of community is to have a digital space where volunteers can connect with each other.
- **A sense of purpose.** Many people go through things in their lives that they don't always share. It feels nice, though, to feel needed and wanted by a group, especially for completing a task or providing one's time in a meaningful way. One of the best examples of this is my friend and volunteer-space mentor, Zubair Talib. He is the CTO of a POS company called Qu. I thought it was particularly appropriate to reference his expertise as a leader of a group of volunteers from around the country. He took the time to learn about volunteers' personal and professional goals and tried to match their volunteer work accordingly.
- **Learning new things.** I remember posting a volunteer role on social media about a year ago, and the overwhelming response I got from people was amazing. The role was for an analytics specialist to look at our community portal's Google Analytics data as well as that of our social media presence. People are leveraging volunteer work to learn new things.

- **A sense of accomplishment.** Every nonprofit or community group is helping someone or some group of people. There is no better satisfaction than that. However, in addition, so many times I have felt like a failure at work but a winner at my volunteer job and have gone to sleep with a smile on my face.

BALANCE ACROSS LOGICAL, EMOTIONAL, AND COOPERATIVE APPEALS

I have sat in on, led, and observed all possible volunteer meetings one can ever be a part of...The topics have ranged from sensitive things like helping a family in need, to tallying finances for an event and making sure all invoices and receipts from a project have been submitted, to strategy sessions to figure out what the future would look like.

These meetings have ebbed and flowed between logical, emotional, and cooperative appeals. Early on in my volunteer career, the modus operandi for leadership was to use emotional appeals. Usually, this volunteer work was part of my religious community center, so there were plenty of opportunities to lead with emotions. And for many years, it worked.

Over time, though, it started taking a toll on me. I needed more than just emotional appeals. I needed to feel like there was more to it than just reminding us of how lucky we were to be immigrants in the first world who had access to so much education and so many resources.

Like, ok. I got it.

Only so many motivational speeches about hungry children or stories of struggling single parents can drive individuals to get tasks done well and on time. Eventually, everyone must feel like whatever small part they are playing contributes, logically, to that greater cause.

This is where it is even more important to tap into one's self-awareness. It seems counter-intuitive to say this, but this is exactly the environment to utilize logical and cooperative appeals the most.

Something that I observed often when working in volunteer environments was that there was a heightened sense of emotions. People were either very grateful to be in that role or felt extremely frustrated because of organizational inefficiencies. However, either way, no one would voice their opinion for fear of hurting someone's pride or feelings or appearing ungrateful for the given opportunity. Alternatively, many of us learned the bad habit of stroking the egos of incompetent leaders and appealing only to the emotions of competent staff members to get things done. This was not enjoyable for me and I had decided to pick and choose how I spent my time volunteering. I saw this happen across a few non-profits that I worked with, as well as community organizations.

This created a highly *imbalanced* work environment. When I started volunteering for the Ismaili Professionals' Network, I was surrounded by professionals and experts from many industries and walks of life. If someone with a background in platforms and systems saw something broken, they felt compelled to say something about it or fix it. I had never volunteered in this environment before and it was exciting. I really felt like I could make a difference with my skills.

What appealed to my colleagues in this volunteer space was understanding the logic or reason behind why we were working on something. They also appreciated being included in brainstorming solutions or working through a problem together. And lastly, there were even some individuals who found their new calling in their career by spending time creating something new in a volunteer environment.

Emotions are always going to be a part of any group or team dynamic. However, knowing the right time and place to utilize emotional appeals is the trick between having a sustainable and effective volunteer organization and one that relies heavily on charismatic leaders to constantly create motivation to work. The latter is not always realistic and can lead to a fizzling out of positive emotions and eventual burnout of volunteers.

KNOWLEDGE-SHARING IS CRITICAL

Turnover within the volunteer space will generally be high. Competing priorities and evolving personal growth objectives will make volunteer work a stop in most people's lives, and not a long-term destination. The fluidity can be embraced as long as mechanisms are set to capture the knowledge and work products generated to be shared with the next person who comes in.

Training is hard to do in a volunteer environment because who is to say there's a right or a wrong way to do something?

If things are documented and shared, there is a starting point for continuity's sake while still leaving room for improvement. The last thing you want is for every volunteer who comes into a role to have to start from scratch.

That would be such a waste of time and resources.

VOLUNTEER WORK: SERVICE AS THE PRIMARY OBJECTIVE

So much of the volunteer work I have done has been in a religious community setting. One thing my family says a lot is, "If you have a chance to serve others, you are blessed." I could have easily made this entire book about the servant leadership style, but I don't think that is for everyone.

As a leader in the volunteer space, everyone should feel like their best self. Some days are more stressful than others, but as a community, we should lift each other up, learn when to ask for help, and communicate with each other why we are there. We can be there for different reasons, as long as we are working toward the same objectives.

CHAPTER 14

WHAT DOES
SUCCESS MEAN?

———

DO AWAY WITH OTHERS' DEFINITION OF SUCCESS

So much of success is linked to our **mindset** and what is
important to us in our sub-conscious. I have met many people who have the title, the money, and the power but are
very unhappy. On the outside, they might not be motivated
by wanting happiness but by wanting validation from their
friends and family by obtaining success in a conventional
sense. This can especially be the case for first-generation children of immigrants. My immigrant family has been consis-
tently looking for financial stability. That is *their* American
dream. But maybe my American dream was based on something different. It took me a while to **anchor myself**.

When I finally obtained a partnership at my first job, I was
happy. Despite all the hostility I experienced from specific
individuals in my work environment, I was finally *somebody*. I was one of the youngest partners, and the first and
only Muslim to be a partner at the twenty-year-old firm. My

parents were finally proud of me for what felt like the first time since I first spoke to them in our family's official language, Gujarati. I was two-and-a-half years old when that happened, so this was a long time coming. My parents told other family members and their friends all about it. I was happy for them. They deserved to be proud of me. Too bad I didn't feel the same way about myself.

Once that initial excitement, and the celebratory dinners, died down, I realized I still had to get up in the morning and face the proverbial music, and it did not sound pretty. In hindsight, it was a cross between the soundtrack of a Trump rally and an Access Hollywood behind the scenes commentary that caused a certain Bush to lose his job. Glad I got out of there when I did.

My definition of success did not match that of some of the people who led that first company in my career (namely the ignorant managing director), so it might have been the right move in the long run to leave the company. My parent's definition of success was not the same as mine either. I did not feel the same way about success as everyone else around me. I did not really know what I was looking for, but I was starting to realize what I did not consider success.

When I joined Accenture, I was a contractor and my title was Research Analyst. In the consulting world, that was basically like starting from the beginning. Had this been five years prior, I would have been bouncing off the walls to be an analyst *at Accenture*. The work that analysts do can get extremely complex quickly. It's work to be proud of. However, I finished college many years ago, I had been working for four or five years and at my most recent major role, I was a partner at a global firm. For me to basically start over at a big company where people my age were at least senior analysts or en route to becoming managers could have been demoralizing.

My close friends who knew I worked at Accenture assumed that I was some big shot since I was going in with some experience. In reality, it wasn't as glamorous as that, at least not when I first started.

The way that position was originally designed, I was supposed to prepare materials for workshops, take notes during workshops, and summarize them afterward in a nice document. It's worth mentioning that they would not have hired me if they had not thought that I could be professional enough in front of very senior level clients (VPs, Directors, C-Suite), so I took that as a compliment.

I worked with many other people who also supported the Innovation Center, and we worked together to make sure things ran smoothly. Eventually, this role turned into so much more. I was researching content for Accenture's innovation centers around the world, learning new workshop facilitation techniques, got to shadow client interviews in preparation for workshops, identified new partnerships for the innovation center, developed relationships with some of those folks, learned about the most cutting edge consumer-facing technologies, and demonstrated them in the center. I was playing with 3D printers and virtual reality equipment and connected fitting rooms and...the list goes on and on. And the people I met from all parts of Accenture and the world, from different industries and backgrounds, were nothing short of amazing.

MY DEFINITION OF SUCCESS AND NO ONE ELSE'S

At first glance, if I had just gone in thinking, "This is not the title I'm looking for," I would have missed out on some of the most fascinating years of my entire career. If I had said, "I don't want to be an analyst because I'm too qualified; I want to be a consultant or senior analyst," I would have missed out on a lot of great experience.

I wanted to share that story about my time with Accenture because what sounded like a glorified workshop assistant eventually turned into something much more where I took pride in everything I did. Every document I created or every workshop that I was a part of was extremely meaningful. The people I worked with every day never made me feel like I was a contractor or somebody at the lower level of the organization's chart. If I had ideas during the workshop in front of the client, they would encourage me to speak up when, in reality, that just would not happen anywhere else. And that spoke volumes of the culture at Accenture.

My time there was more than just a paycheck. It was a place **where I could measure success by how much my knowledge bank was growing. I started to learn what it meant to truly have a growth mindset—not just in theory but in practice. I disrupted other's definition of my success and evolved my own definition.** I was in grad school at the same time, getting my master's in integrated marketing communications.

I would read things in books or hear something in class and then see it happen at a real-life company the next day at work.

At Accenture and IRC, I could sit in a room with C-level executives of Fortune 500 and Fortune 1000 companies on a daily or weekly basis. Now, it wasn't just about being around these important people but also about being in the room as they made major decisions about the future of their organization.

HOLISTIC MEASURES OF SUCCESS

Success is often measured in monetary or status gains. Those are definitely measures that can be tangibly seen and easy to track toward. However, simply having more money or getting a higher title cannot ensure the growth in mindset that can occur by obtaining meaningful experiences. In my less-than-fifteen years of work experience, I have gotten the titles and obtained monetary success, but I also simultaneously experienced high levels of stress and loneliness, low levels of genuine happiness, no sense of purpose at times, and feeling like I was not creating value.

On the outside, I looked like a winner, but on the inside, I felt empty at many levels. I gained the wisdom to focus on a more holistic measure of success.

Additionally, not just as a leader but as a person, I communicate what success means to me so that everyone around me is marching to the same beat. If they do not agree or do not see eye-to-eye about what I consider success, I can get a sense of it right away. I know who to include in my inner circle and who not to include. There is no need to feel obligated to engage with people who could sabotage my sense of purpose and happiness.

For me, long-term measures of success can be principles of success that can apply to one's personal life and their professional/business life. They are linked. Organize life in such a way to aim for balance across these areas. There isn't always a way to achieve success in every area all the time, but these are high level enough to be relevant to whatever your personal or professional goals might be:

- Financial stability/sustainability – **Strategically**, this will help keep other areas stable, but putting all your focus here can cause unnecessary risks in the other areas noted below.
- Mental health
- Prioritizing **people** important to you (family, friends, co-workers, mentors, etc.)
    - Spend quality time with them.
    - Work on having a relationship with them that is:
        - Healthy for you
        - Healthy for them
    - Surround yourself with people who are in it for the long haul, not immediate gratification.
- Continue to be motivated by the good in the world:
    - Your purpose in life can be whatever you want it to be but believe in goodness.
    - Contribute to the goodness in the world.
    - Use your [**super**] **power** to inspire others to do the same.

There are many labels and mindsets that we need to shake in order to realign to our own vision of the future. How we define success and communicating it to those around us can allow us to achieve our intended success. Having power or wealth is not a long-lasting success metric; you can have these one day and then not have it another day. How you use power and resources to empower yourself and others can be turned into a true sense of purpose and fulfillment.

APPENDIX

INTRODUCTION

Ames, Daniel R., and Lara K. Kammrath. "Mind-Reading and Metacognition: Narcissism, not Actual Competence, Predicts Self-Estimated Ability." Columbia.edu. Access date 4/25/2020.

Connley, Courtney. 2019. "The Number of Women Running Fortune 500 Companies Is at a Record High." CNBC. May 16, 2019. https://www.cnbc.com/2019/05/16/the-number-of-women-running-fortune-500-companies-is-at-a-record-high.html.

Kruger, Justin, and Dunning, David. "Unskilled and Unaware of It: How Difficulties in Recognizing One's Own Incompetence Lead to Inflated Self-Assessments." *Journal of Personality and Social Psychology*, 77 (6) (1999): 1121–1134.

Singh, Lilly. *How to Be a Bawse*. New York: Random House, 2017.

CHAPTER 1

Abulof, Uriel, "What Is the Arab Third Estate?" HuffPost, December 7, 2017. https://www.huffpost.com/entry/what-is-the-arab-third-es_b_832628.

Gander, Kashmira. "550 Years Since Niccolo Machiavelli Was Born—How to Check How Machiavellian You Are." *Newsweek.* May 3, 2019. https://www.newsweek.com/550-years-niccolo-machiavelli-was-born-how-check-how-machiavellian-you-are-1408155.

Harari, Yuval Noah. *Sapiens: A Brief History of Humankind.* Canada: Harper Perennial, 2014.

"Master the 3 Ways to Influence People." Center for Creative Leadership. Accessed April 25, 2020. https://www.ccl.org/articles/leading-effectively-articles/three-ways-to-influence/.

Merriam-Webster. s.v. "Machiavellianism (_n._)." Accessed July 27, 2020. https://www.merriam-webster.com/dictionary/Machiavellianism.

Popovic, Srdja. *Blueprint for Revolution: How to Use Rice Pudding, Lego Men, and Other Nonviolent Techniques to Galvanize Communities, Overthrow Dictators, or Simply Change the World.* New York: Random House Publishing Group, 2015. Kindle.

Weber, Eugen, *Movements, Currents, Trends: Aspects of European Thought in the Nineteenth and Twentieth Centuries,* 1992.

CHAPTER 2

Gilbert, Elizabeth. *Eat, Pray, Love*. London: Bloomsbury Publishing, 2007.

King, Jamilah, Inae Oh, and Kiera Butler. "Oprah's Book Club Changed the Game—and Created a New World for Black Readers Like Me." Mother Jones. Nov. 1, 2019. https://www.motherjones.com/media/2019/11/oprah-book-club-apple-tv-plus-relaunch-legacy-black-writers/.

CHAPTER 3

Agarwal, Pragya. "Unconscious Bias: Do Women Discriminate Against Women?" LinkedIn, March 1, 2018. https://www.linkedin.com/pulse/unconscious-bias-do-women-discriminate-against-pragya-agarwal/.

Albright, Madeleine. Keynote speech at Celebrating Inspiration luncheon with the WNBA's All-Decade Team, ESPN.com, 2006, accessed July 27, 2020. https://www.espn.com/wnba/columns/story?columnist=voepel_mechelle&id=2517642.

Beard, Mary. *Women & Power*. New York: Liveright Publishing, 2017.

Chamorro-Premuzic, Tomas. *Why Do So Many Incompetent Men Become Leaders: And How To Fix It*. Boston: Harvard Business School Publishing, 2019.

Clark, Dorie. "If Strategy Is So Important, Why Don't We Make Time for It?" *Harvard Business Review*, June 21, 2018. https://hbr.org/2018/06/if-strategy-is-so-important-why-dont-we-make-time-for-it.

Lakhani, Sabrina. "Birthing a New Consciousness" (blog), May 25, 2016. https://sabrinalakhani.com/relationships/birthing-a-new-consciousness/.

Namie, Gary. "2017 WBI U.S. Workplace Bullying Survey." Workplace Bullying Institute. Accessed April 25, 2020. https://www.workplacebullying.org/multi/img/2017/Infographic-2017.png.

CHAPTER 4

Merriam-Webster. s.v. "entrepreneur (_n._)." Accessed July 26, 2020. https://www.merriam-webster.com/dictionary/entrepreneur.

CHAPTER 5

Indivero, Victoria M. "Think Twice, Speak Once: Bilinguals Process Both Languages." Penn State University, September 10, 2013. https://news.psu.edu/story/286926/2013/09/10/research/think-twice-speak-once-bilinguals-process-both-languages.

CHAPTER 6

Dweck, Carol. *Mindset: The New Psychology of Success.* New York: Penguin House, 2016.

"Narendra Modi's Sectarianism Is Eroding India's Secular Democracy." *Economist,* January 23, 2020. Accessed July 26, 2020. https://www.economist.com/briefing/2020/01/23/narendra-modis-sectarianism-is-eroding-indias-secular-democracy.

CHAPTER 7

Emsi. "Emerging Jobs & Skills in STEM." Economic Modeling Specialists International, April 2017. https://www.economic-modeling.com/emerging-jobs-and-skills-in-stem/.

Goleman, Daniel. "What Makes A Leader?" in *HBR's 10 Must Reads On Leadership, 1-21.* Boston: Harvard Business School Publishing, 2011.

Kalil, Tom. Jahanian, Farnam. "Computer Science is for Everyone!" The White House President Barack Obama. Archives, December 2013. https://obamawhitehouse.archives.gov/blog/2013/12/11/computer-science-everyone

Strauss, Valerie. "The Surprising Thing Google Learned about Its Employees — And What It Means for Today's Students." *The Washington Post*, Dec. 20, 2017. https://www.washingtonpost.com/news/answer-sheet/wp/2017/12/20/the-surprising-thing-google-learned-about-its-employees-and-what-it-means-for-todays-students/.

CHAPTER 9

Clark, Dorie. "If Strategy Is So Important, Why Don't We Make Time for It?" *Harvard Business Review*, June 21, 2018. https://hbr.org/2018/06/if-strategy-is-so-important-why-dont-we-make-time-for-it.

Department of Sociology - Northwestern University, "Ethnography," Accessed April 25, 2020. https://www.sociology.north-western.edu/about/events/workshops/ethnography.html.

CHAPTER 10

Columbus, Louis. "IBM Predicts Demand for Data Scientists Will Soar 28% by 2020." *Forbes*, May 13, 2017. https://www.forbes.com/sites/louiscolumbus/2017/05/13/ibm-predicts-demand-for-data-scientists-will-soar-28-by-2020/#680dc06a7e3b

CHAPTER 11

Kotter, John P. A Force For Change: How Leadership Differs From Management. New York: Free Press, 1990.

Kotter, John. "What Leaders Really Do," in *HBR's 10 Must Reads On Leadership*. Boston: Harvard Business School Publishing, 2011.

CHAPTER 13

The.Ismaili. "The Ismaili Community." Accessed April 25, 2020. https://the.ismaili/global/about-us/the-ismaili-community.